TAYBA

ISLAM 98 FOUNDATIONS OF ISLAM

TAYBA FOUNDATION

Edited by: Sheima Sumer, Umm Ahmed, and Rami Nsour
Content development: Nusayba Elqabbany
Proofreading: Kelly Legere-Gallant
Graphic design and cover: Monica Saldana

We would like to thank our generous donors. Their support makes a coursebook such as this possible. Please keep them in your prayers.

Islamic Calligraphy used with permission from FreeIslamicCalligraphy.com.

Table of Contents

Tayba Foundation & what we stand for

At the Tayba Foundation, we believe that all people contain a wellspring of goodness within them, and we believe in the power of human potential.

Even when individuals encounter dramatic setbacks in life, lasting change is possible.

Tayba Foundation is a non-profit organization dedicated to serving individuals and families impacted by incarceration. We believe in the power of human change through holistic education, guidance, and support.

The Essentials program for Islamic studies

The Tayba Essentials program includes the most important things for you to know about Islam, and to practice. This is a CORRESPONDENCE COURSE.

ISLAM98: *Foundations of Islam* is the first course in the Essentials program.

Tayba's Curriculum Path

1	2	3	4
Essentials Track *Average of 18+ months*	**Intermediate Track** *Average of 5+ years*	**Arabic Language Studies**	**Advanced Track Course**
8 foundational courses with essential information for every Muslim, in easy-to-read texts in color, with many opportunities to check one's understanding. Courses include enrichment and reflection exercises.	Course List: Aqida (IMAN 100, 101) Fiqh (FIQH 100, 101, 102) Adab (ADAB 100, 101, 102) Sira 101 Qur'an 101 Usul 101 Hadith 101 Iman 101	Arabic Studies program offers learning from the very beginner level (Arabic alphabet) to intermediate Arabic, including assessments.	Course List: 'Aqida (Iman 201) Ihsan 201 Individualized further study

Course Schedule: How to work through this coursebook

The Essentials courses are to be taken at your own pace, there are no semesters or terms. This means that you, the learner, will work your way through this book and the exercises in your own time. Every learner is different, though we recommend that everyone take at least 2 months to read this book in detail and bring it into your life. These coursebooks are NOT designed to be rushed, so take your time and enjoy the journey!

When you have done that, **complete the end reflection at the back of this book.** Carefully tear out the two pages ONLY and send those to us.

Tayba mailing address:

TAYBA FOUNDATION
PO Box 1154
Portsmouth NH 03802

How to get in touch if you have questions

If you need to understand something that is in this book better, you can ask us questions about the content of this coursebook. We receive a lot of questions so please be patient as we try to answer them all.

Note that due to the number of letters we receive, we are not always able to answer questions that are not about this coursebook.

By e-mail: Email us at **instructors@taybafoundation.org**
When sending e-mail, always include "ISLAM98 Foundations of Islam" in the subject line of the message.

By letter: Include on the envelope "ISLAM98 Foundations of Islam". This will help us to respond to your letter more quickly.

Please be sure to write your name and prison ID clearly on all communications so we know it's from you and can reply to you. If you move facility, please let us know as soon as possible so we know where to reach you.

Tayba mailing address:

TAYBA FOUNDATION
PO Box 1154
Portsmouth NH 03802

Course Updates

This book, Islam 98 Foundations of Islam, replaces Islam 99 Introduction to Islam.

This is now the first book in the Tayba Essentials program. If you already have Islam 99 Introduction to Islam, you will see that:

1. The content has been updated
2. There are additional chapters covering the topic of Ihsan, which are essential reading for every Muslim
3. There are new reflection exercises

What to do when you have finished working through this book

The end reflection exercise is at the back of this book. You must return it to us at the address above. Do not send the other questions or exercises back to Tayba: only the one at the back of the book. The point of this book is to help you to learn and practice your religion. The exercise we ask for is meant to be helpful to you and also allows us to see how much you have learned.

You cannot fail this exercise but if it is clear you have struggled with it, we may ask you to read through the book again and attempt it again.

Carefully tear out the two end reflection pages, complete them and send us the pages. Another way is to write out your answers on a separate sheet of paper if you prefer.

When we receive the reflection pages* we will mail the next course book in the Essentials program to you. Please allow up to 45 days for the next book to be mailed to you. We will NOT return your reflection exercise.

May Allah bless you on your journey and grant you success in your studies. Ameen.

* Please note: In order to protect the personal and private information of our students, our policy is to shred all documents using a secure shredding service once it has been processed. This includes application forms, course assessments and letters.

An important note about the contents of this book

Allah says in the Quran, **"And whoever honors the sacred things of Allah, it is better for him with his Lord." Quran 22:30.**

What is Sacred? When it comes to things written down, this includes: verses of the Quran, Hadith (sayings of the Prophet, Allah bless him and grant him peace), the 99 Names of Allah; the names of the Prophets and the Angels (Allah bless them one and all). This book contains Sacred texts in both Arabic and English.

How should I honor them?

- Avoid placing them on the ground and do not sit on them, rest feet etc.
- Try to keep them from getting damaged beyond regular wear and tear.
- If possible, keep them away from people who may be disrespectful.
- Avoid placing anything on top of the Quran and religious books in general.

I need to dispose of a book or piece of paper with Sacred text on it. How can I do that in prison?

Throwing them in the trash or recycle bin is considered disrespectful and is not allowed. We suggest that you do *one* of the following:

First method:
- **Step 1:** Tear / cut out the section that has the Sacred text. For example, if it is one verse from the Quran at the top of a page, tear or cut out that top part. There is no need to dispose of the full page or the full book.
- **Step 2:** Manually (with your hands) shred the paper into very small pieces so that the words can no longer be made out.
- **Step 3:** Put the shredded paper into the recycling (if possible) so that it does not mix with anything dirty. What is left of the book or piece of paper can also go into the recycling.

Second method:
Erase the words by soaking the paper in water until the paper turns to pulp and the writing can no longer be read.

Third method:
Mail the material to us at our Union City address. We will dispose of it correctly for you. If you do this, **make sure to tell us this is for disposing.** Or mail it to someone else on the outside with instructions on how to dispose of it.

Introduction to Islam

MAIN POINTS

- Islam 98 will summarize the fundamentals needed to believe in, and practice Islam.
- The Hadith of Jibril tells us the four components of the deen of Islam.

LEARNING OBJECTIVES

- To name and describe the Quran and the Sunnah and explain their importance in Islam.
- To identify the four components of the deen according to the Hadith of Jibril.

Reflection Questions

- In what ways does Islam make your life have a purpose?
- What are your main reasons for wanting to learn more about Islam?

Key Terms

- **Prophet Muhammad:** The last Messenger of Allah. He conveyed Allah's final, untouched message of Oneness
- **ﷺ:** Every time the Prophet Muhammad ﷺ is mentioned, we send peace and blessings upon him. This symbol is the Arabic term
- **Deen:** religion, complete way of life
- **Islam:** submission to Allah
- **Iman:** faith
- **Ihsan:** spiritual excellence
- **As-Sa'a:** End of Time/Final Hour
- **Hadith of Jibril:** authentic narration of the Angel Gabriel asking the Prophet Muhammad ﷺ about the components of the deen of Islam

Introduction to Islam

You are a noble person. Allah bestowed nobility upon humans like no other of His creation. Allah tells us in the Quran:

❴ **We have honored the Children of Adam** ❵
Quran 17:70

As you pick up this book and begin reading these lines, you are using the nobility and honor Allah has given you: hands, eyes, intellect, and many other blessings.

What are some other ways Allah has honored humanity?

-

-

-

This book aims to summarize some of the main concepts of *Islam.* We learn about Islam through the Quran and Sunnah.

The Quran is the final revelation from Allah. It is the words of Allah and tells us who Allah is, how to strengthen our connection to Him, and our rights and responsibilities as His servants.

The Sunnah is the preserved narrations of everything the *Prophet Muhammad, peace be upon him* (ﷺ), said, did, or affirmed. This is how we learn the details of our worship, and how to behave as Muslims.

Some scholars dedicate their entire lives to studying specific branches of the Quran and Sunnah.

Hundreds of thousands of Muslims go on Pilgrimage every year. This is one part of upholding the teachings of the Quran and Sunnah.

This way of faith and living is Islam. It is the same Islam that all the prophets and messengers of Allah followed.

Islam: A Complete Way of Life

Allah tells us in the Quran,

❨ **Certainly, Allah's only Way [deen] is Islam [full submission to Allah].** ❩
Quran 3:19

Deen can be translated as "religion," but it is also more wholly translated as "a complete way of life." This verse says that the only way of life, or religion, that Allah will recognize is complete submission to Allah.

Islam means to submit to Allah.

We submit to Allah by doing our best to please Him and follow the example of His Prophet Muhammad ﷺ. We do this by understanding why we worship Allah, who He and His Messenger Muhammad ﷺ are, and by doing our best to do what He has commanded us to do and avoid what He has prohibited. Islam is a life-long journey where we are constantly trying to learn and better ourselves.

All the previous Prophets and Messengers brought the same "deen" of Islam because they brought the same belief system. All Messengers taught their followers complete submission to Allah. However, there was a difference in their systems of law, known as shari'a. Shari'a tells us how to pray, fast, etc.

Each Prophet or Messenger either followed a previously revealed shari'a or was given his own. While the shari'as of the Prophets may have differed, they all came with the same belief system.

Each Prophet sent by Allah reaffirmed what the previous Prophets brought in terms of belief. Their laws may have differed, but the final law given to the Prophet Muhammad ﷺ is now the only law that we follow.

Our Deen has four important components:

→ **Islam** (submission to Allah),
→ **Iman** (faith),
→ **Ihsan** (spiritual excellence),
→ and knowing some of the signs of **As-Sa'a** (the final hour/ End of Time).

Circle the names of the components as you read the hadith on the next page.

Hadith of Jibril

'Umar ibn Al-Khattab reported: One day, we were sitting with the Messenger of Allah ﷺ, and a man appeared with very white clothes and very black hair. There were no signs of travel on him and we did not recognize him. He sat in front of the Prophet ﷺ, put his knees to his knees and his hands on his thighs and said, "O Muhammad! Tell me about Islam."

The Messenger of Allah ﷺ said, "Islam is to testify that there is no God but Allah and Muhammad is His Messenger; to establish prayer; to pay zakat [money due to the poor]; to fast the month of Ramadan; and to perform pilgrimage to the House if a way is possible."

The man said, "You have spoken the truth." We were surprised at his questioning him (the Messenger ﷺ) and then telling him he was right. He went on to say, "Tell me about faith (iman)."

The Messenger of Allah ﷺ answered, "It is that you believe in Allah, His Angels, His Books, His Messengers, in the Last Day, and in Qadr (fate)—both in its good and in its evil aspects."

The man said, "You have spoken the truth." Then the man said, "Tell me about spiritual excellence (ihsan)."

The Messenger of Allah ﷺ said, "It is that you should worship Allah as if you can see Him, for though you cannot see Him, [know that] He sees you."

The man said, "Tell me about the Final Hour (As-Sa'a)."

The Messenger ﷺ said, "The one asked does not know more than the one asking."

The man said, "Tell me about its signs."

The Prophet ﷺ said, "The slave-girl will give birth to her mistress, and that you will see the barefoot, naked, destitute shepherds compete in the construction of tall buildings."

Then the man left and I remained. The Prophet ﷺ said to me, "O, 'Umar, do you know who he was?"

I said, "Allah and His Messenger know best."

He ﷺ said, "That was Jibril (the Angel Gabriel). He came to teach you your religion (deen)." (Narrated by Muslim)

The 4 Components of Our Deen

This hadith is known as the Hadith of Jibril. A hadith is an authentic narration that tells us what the Prophet ﷺ said, did, or affirmed. In it, "deen" is described by the Messenger of Allah ﷺ as having four components: Islam, Iman, Ihsan, and signs of As-Sa'a. Under the topic of Islam, there are five pillars; under the topic of Iman, there are six pillars; under the topic of Ihsan, there are two pillars; and under the topic of As-Sa'a, there are two signs.

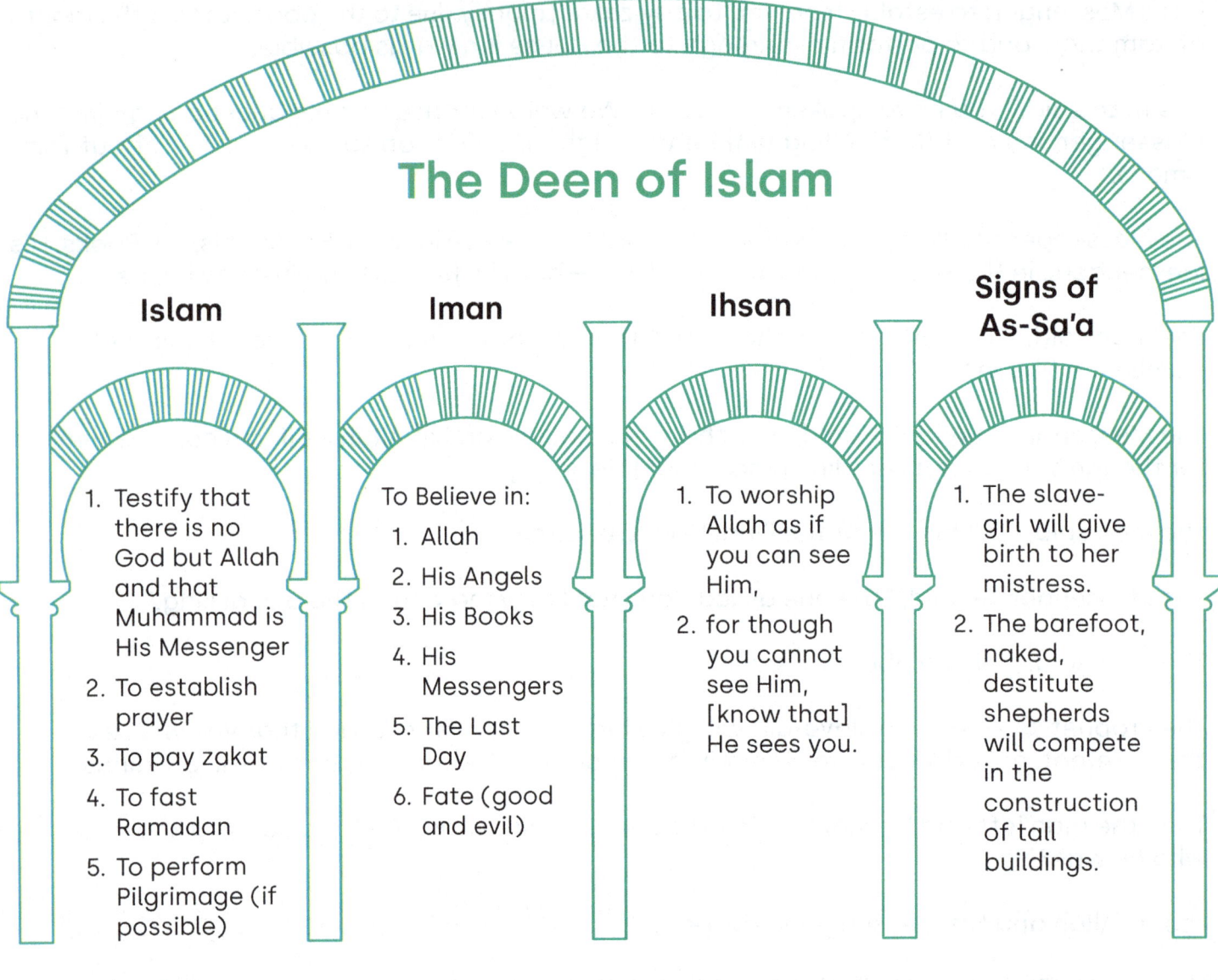

The Deen of Islam

Islam

1. Testify that there is no God but Allah and that Muhammad is His Messenger
2. To establish prayer
3. To pay zakat
4. To fast Ramadan
5. To perform Pilgrimage (if possible)

Iman

To Believe in:
1. Allah
2. His Angels
3. His Books
4. His Messengers
5. The Last Day
6. Fate (good and evil)

Ihsan

1. To worship Allah as if you can see Him,
2. for though you cannot see Him, [know that] He sees you.

Signs of As-Sa'a

1. The slave-girl will give birth to her mistress.
2. The barefoot, naked, destitute shepherds will compete in the construction of tall buildings.

Our deen is vast and covers every aspect of life. The goal of this book is to present a simple introduction to the four components of deen as a critical first step to learning about Islam.

This book will also contain material which is important when beginning on the path of Islamic education in the prison context. We pray that Allah makes all of us from those who have a sound understanding of deen because the Messenger of Allah ﷺ said: "When Allah wishes good for someone, He gives him/her the understanding of deen." (Bukhari, Muslim)

Introduction to Islam

1. What is the Quran?

2. What is the Sunnah?

Circle True or False.

1 We submit to Allah by doing what pleases Him.   **True / False**

2 We don't have to follow the Sunnah.   **True / False**

3 Islam is a life-long journey.   **True / False**

4 All prophets taught their followers to submit to Allah.   **True / False**

There are 4 components of this Deen. Which component is this from?

Islam   : prayer

           : fasting

           : belief in the angels

           : to worship Allah as if you see Him

           : The barefoot, naked, destitute shepherds will compete in the construction of tall buildings.

Introduction to Islam

What are some ways that Islam is a complete way of life (deen)?

Why is understanding of the deen a gift from Allah?

What are some of the most important things you learned/reviewed in this chapter?

This is an optional section.
Completing it is not necessary for the successful completion of this book.

Muslims Around the World

Islam is a religion for all people, from all backgrounds. The Prophet ﷺ said in his farewell sermon, "An Arab has no superiority over a non-Arab, nor does a non-Arab have any superiority over an Arab...except by piety and good action." The Quran states that one of Allah's signs is:

❮ **the diversity of your languages and colors.** ❯
Quran 30:22

→ **Top 5 Countries with the largest number of Muslims**

Rank	Country	Muslims	Total Population
1	Indonesia	243,577,186	279,973,776
2	Pakistan	236,971,732	245,566,562
3	India	222,180,838	1,442,732,712
4	Bangladesh	158,751,333	174,836,270
5	Nigeria	117,301,109	229,552,071

→ **Muslim Population by Region**

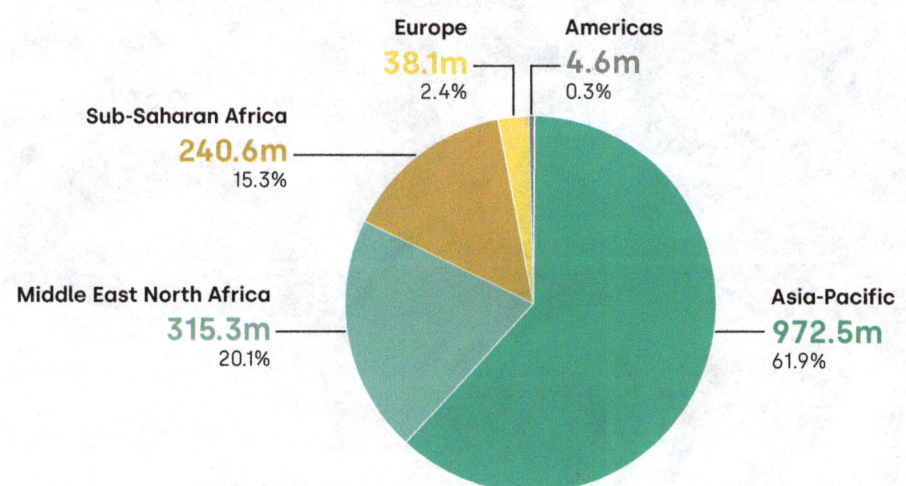

As you can see from the charts, most Muslims are non-Arab. There are about 2 billion Muslims in the world. 13% of Muslims are from Indonesia.

→ Muslims around the World

Muslims at a masjid in Nairobi, Kenya

Muslims praying Eid Prayer in Rawalpindi, Pakistan

Muslims at a masjid in the United Arab Emirates

Muslims praying in a masjid in Maryland, USA

Muslims making tawaf at the Kaaba in Makkah

The 5 Pillars of Islam

MAIN POINTS

- The 5 pillars of Islam are Shahada, Prayer, Zakah, Fasting, and Pilgrimage.
- Shahada is the first pillar of Islam and is the declaration of faith.

LEARNING OBJECTIVES

- To identify the 5 pillars of Islam
- To demonstrate understanding of the Shahada

Reflection Questions

- What made you want to practice Islam?
- In what ways has practicing Islam benefitted you?

Key Terms

- **Shahada:** declaration of faith
- **Salah:** the daily prayers
- **Zakah:** obligatory alms
- **Sawm:** fasting
- **Hajj:** pilgrimage to Makkah
- **Munafiq:** hypocrite

The 5 Pillars of Islam

In chapter 1, we covered the 4 components of deen. In this chapter, we will cover the first component: Islam. Islam means submission to Allah. We submit to Allah by obeying His commands and avoiding what He has prohibited.

The five most important acts of worship Allah has commanded us to do are called "The Pillars of Islam." Just as pillars keep a building strong and sturdy, the pillars of Islam uphold our Islam. If a pillar is missing, the building is still standing, but has become weakened. Similarly, if a pillar of Islam is missing in our practice, our Islam is weakened.

Consider what would happen if one of these pillars was damaged or demolished entirely.

The Messenger of Allah ﷺ said, "Islam is to declare that there is no God but Allah and Muhammad is His Messenger, to establish prayer, to pay the obligatory alms, to fast the month of Ramadan, and to perform pilgrimage to the House if a way is possible." (Bukhari)

The above hadith tells us the 5 pillars of Islam:
1. The declaration of faith *(shahada)*
2. The five daily prayers *(salah)*
3. Paying the obligatory alms *(zakah)*
4. Fasting the month of Ramadan *(sawm)*
5. Pilgrimage to the House [the Kaaba in Makkah] *(hajj)*

The First Pillar: The Declaration of Faith (Shahada)

The shahada is the verbal declaration that enters one into Islam. It is commonly transliterated as:

Ash-hadu an laa ilaha illa-Llah, wa ash-hadu anna Muhammada-r-Rasoolullah

"I bear witness that there is no God but Allah, and I bear witness that Muhammad ﷺ is the Messenger of Allah."

A piece of Arabic calligraphy with the Shahada on it. This specific piece resembles the fabric covering the outside of the grave of the Prophet Muhammad ﷺ in Madinah. The original letters are sewn with gold thread.

→ Its Significance

Saying "Ash-hadu an laa ilaha illa-Llah" is to recognize the One God (Allah) as the only One you worship and pray to.

Saying "Ash-hadu anna Muhammada-r-Rasoolullah" is to recognize that Muhammad ﷺ is the final Prophet and Messenger.

→ Why must one say the shahada?

A person says the shahada in front of other Muslim witnesses so that the community knows they are Muslim. It also allows the community to fulfill the obligations due to fellow Muslims. If someone tells us they are Muslim, we believe them.

It's important to note that if a person believes exactly what Muslims believe, but has not formally spoken the shahada to other Muslims, he or she is still considered to be Muslim by Allah, as long as there was some verbal testimony of faith on their part, even in private.

→ Does the shahada have to be stated in Arabic?

The shahada can be said in any language, and it can be done in any place. Once a person accepts Islam, all their previous sins are erased.

If a person is asked in any language if he/she believes in one God, His Messengers, His Books, His Angels, the Last Day and The Decree of God and each article of belief is clarified with regards to negating their former beliefs and the person answer "Yes", that counts as a shadada. This person is now Muslim.

→ Can a person be Muslim and not practice?

While it's very important that Muslims practice their faith through actions, faith itself is not dependent on practice.

Here is a hadith that clearly proves that someone who does not practice will still be considered a Muslim:

Ubada Ibn Samit [a companion] narrates that the Messenger of Allah ﷺ said, "Allah has ordained upon His servant five daily prayers. Whoever performs them and does not abandon them, then for him is Allah's promise to enter Paradise. Whosoever doesn't perform them, then he doesn't have the promise from Allah. Thus, if Allah wills, He will punish him. If He wills, He will forgive him." (Muwatta, Abu Dawud)

Thousands of Muslims gathering together to pray

Some people believe that not praying immediately takes a person out of Islam. It is clear from this hadith that someone who doesn't pray but still believes the prayer to be obligatory is still a Muslim.

Keep this hadith in mind when you encounter non-practicing Muslims, or people who are thinking about entering Islam but are hesitating because they don't feel ready to practice.

The person may say, "I don't want to be a hypocrite, and I want to practice fully if I become Muslim." You may tell them that they will not be a hypocrite *(munafiq)*. The definition of a munafiq is one who outwardly professes and practices Islam, but inwardly does not believe in Islam. This is different than a person who inwardly accepts Islam, outwardly professes it, and yet has some struggles in practicing Islam.

Secondly, remind them that we never know when our life will end, and it is better to end in a state of having declared Islam.

With the blessing of the declaration of faith (shahada), the person will be given the strength to practice.

→   Can a person delay the shahada?

It is important not to delay saying the shahada.

Once a person is willing to pronounce the shahada after understanding it, no one should ever encourage him/her to delay it even for a minute. Asking a person to delay the shahada is like saying, "You should remain in disbelief for a little longer!"

A person must say their shahada as soon as they believe in Islam. One should not delay a single instant – even if alone. One can repeat it again in front of a Muslim congregation.

The 5 Pillars of Islam

Write the name of the pillar of Islam.

_____ : a phrase you declare to let others know you are Muslim.

_____ : Muslims do this five times a day.

_____ : Muslims do this in the month of Ramadan.

Circle True or False.

1	Once a person makes a statement of faith in Islam, we should investigate and figure out if that person is indeed a Muslim.	True / False
2	If a person says that he/she is a Muslim, that is enough for us to treat them as Muslim and offer them all the rights they are owed.	True / False
3	If a person believes exactly what Muslims believe, but has not formally spoken the shahada, he or she is still considered to be Muslim with Allah.	True / False
4	If a person says the shahada without understanding the words or believing the meaning, he or she is still considered to be a Muslim by Allah.	True / False
5	The shahada can be said in any language, and it can be done in any place.	True / False
6	A Muslim who struggles with their 5 daily prayers is no longer a Muslim.	True / False

Why is it important for a person to not delay in saying their shahada?

_____

_____

_____

The 5 Pillars of Islam

If you have said the Shahada, how did you feel?

Did you know that we say the Shahada in every prayer? Why do you think this may be?

What are some of the most important things you learned/reviewed in this chapter?

This is an optional section.
Completing it is not necessary for the successful completion of this book.

Masjids Around the World – Art Therapy

Copy/draw, decorate or color this masjid while learning about it.

Al Masjid Al Haram, Makkah

We pray in the direction of the Ka'ba. It was originally built by Prophet Ibrahim and his son, Prophet Isma'il. Millions of Muslims visit it every year. Masjid al-Haram, the sacred masjid surrounding the Ka'ba, is one of the holiest sites in Islam.

Art by: Malcolme Morgan, Tayba student

Preparation for Prayer (Salah)

MAIN POINTS

- Prayer Is the most important act of worship in Islam.
- Prayer prevents sins and evils.
- A person must be in a state of ritual purity before they pray.
- Minor ritual impurity is removed by doing wudu. Major ritual impurity is removed by doing ghusl.
- Tayammum is a way to ritually purify oneself when water is not available.

LEARNING OBJECTIVES

- To know the importance of prayer
- To recognize types of physical impurity
- To identify causes of minor ritual impurity and major ritual impurity
- To know when wudu and ghusl are needed
- To understand how to perform wudu, ghusl, and tayammum

Reflection Questions

- Have you ever done your wudu? How did you feel the first time you performed wudu (ritual washing before prayer)?
- How does praying give you strength throughout your day?

Key Terms

- **Najasa:** filth
- **Wudu:** ritual washing
- **Tahara:** ritual purity/cleanliness
- **Ghusl:** ritual shower
- **Fard:** required
- **Sunnah:** recommended
- **Tayammum:** dry ritual purification

Prayer (Salah)

After understanding the importance of the Shahada in the five pillars, we move onto the next pillar: Prayer. Prayer is the most important act of worship in Islam.

It is the proof of true belief in Allah. The main purpose of prayer is to fill our hearts with an awareness of the greatness of Allah. It also helps us to gain the pleasure and Mercy of Allah.

Prayer helps us to avoid acts of disobedience and can cleanse us from past minor ones. Although the prayer looks like a simple action, once established with love for Allah and His Messenger ﷺ in our hearts, it can have transformative effects.

The Quran says,

⟨**...Indeed, prayer deters ˹one˺ from indecency and wickedness....**⟩
Quran 29:45

The Messenger of Allah ﷺ said, "The five daily prayers can be likened to an overflowing river of sweet water which flows by someone's door and rushes into the house five times a day. How much filth do you think it will leave in that house?"

In response, his listeners replied, "None!" "So it is," he told them. "The five daily prayers wash away sins just as water washes away dirt and filth." (Bukhari)

We must prepare for such an important act. Just as you would prepare to meet someone very important to you, you must prepare even more when you are going to address your Lord, Allah.

Preparation

Preparing for prayer includes:

- Physical purity: making sure that our bodies, clothes, and places of prayer are free of impurities.
- Ritual purity: Washing for prayer - This is different than removing impurity.
- Preparing our hearts: to make sure we're focused, and in the right frame of mind.

1. **Physical Purity:** Preparing our bodies, clothes and the place where we pray. This is done by removing physical impurity. Impurity *(najasa)* is clearly defined in Islam. Physical impurity (najasa) includes the presence of:

   - Blood, pus, or vomit (unless in very small amounts)
   - Urine or feces
   - Carcasses of animals not properly slaughtered (meat that is not halal or kosher)
   - Liquid intoxicants (beer, wine, pruno)

Any of these need to be washed from your body, clothing, and the area where you will pray.

2. **Ritual Purity:** The state of ritual purity *(tahara)* is achieved in one of two ways, depending on one's situation. This type of purity is not related to removing impurities. Ritual purity involves performing specific acts before prayer.

The Virtues of Ritual Purity (Tahara)

Ritual purity has many benefits:

- Ritual purity (tahara) removes minor sins from the believer.
- Washing before prayer helps to focus the heart and the intention of the person on their goal, which is to worship Allah.
- Washing removes laziness and fatigue.
- Cleanliness is from the station of spiritual excellence, and Allah loves those who keep themselves clean.
- Ritual purity will manifest as light on the day of judgment.
- Cleanliness is half of faith (iman), and faith leads to Paradise.

Methods of Ritual Purity

1. The first method of ritual purity is called ritual washing (wudu). Wudu is a set method of washing certain parts of the body to achieve the state of purity.

2. The second method is called ritual showering **(ghusl)**. Ghusl is to wash the entire body to achieve the state of purity.

Both ritual washing (wudu) and ritual showering (ghusl) require clean water and to make sure that there is no substance on the skin that prevents the water from reaching it. This can include nail polish, grease, or paint. One must remove any substances that form a layer on the skin before washing or showering. (There is an exception for medical substances such as casts, wraps, or stitches.)

1. Wudu:

If the following below exist, then this person is in a state of minor ritual impurity. This would require a minor ritual washing (wudu) before a person can pray. A person is required to have wudu for all of the five prayers.

Minor ritual impurity is caused by:

1. Urinating, defecating, or passing gas
2. Loss of consciousness or deep sleep
3. Intoxication or states of insanity
4. Lustful emission of pre-ejaculatory fluid
5. Sensual touching and kissing
6. Touching the private parts with the palm or fingers

How to Perform Ritual Washing (Wudu)

The Messenger of Allah ﷺ said,

"Ritual washing (wudu) is the key to salah."

(Tirmidhi)

Allah says,

❴O believers! When you rise up for prayer, wash your faces and
your hands up to the elbows, wipe your heads, and wash your feet to the
ankles. And if you are in a state of ˹full˺ impurity, then take a full bath.❵
Quran 5:6

Intention

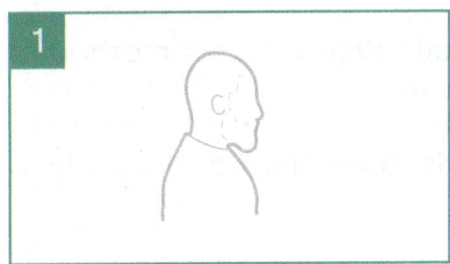

Action: Make the intention to perform ritual washing (wudu), while saying, "Bismillah."

Number of times: x 1

Ruling: intention is <u>required</u>, saying "Bismillah" is recommended

Hands

Action: Wash both hands up to and including the wrist, starting with the right. Make sure to clean in between the fingers.

Number of times: x 3

Ruling: recommended

Mouth

Action: Take water into your mouth with your right hand and rinse it out making sure you swish the water around.

Number of times: x 3

Ruling: recommended

Nose

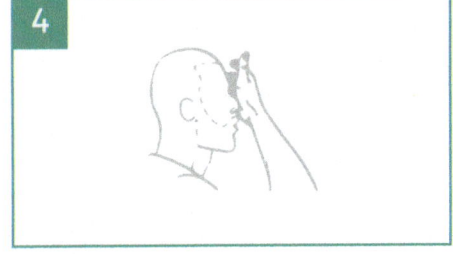

Action: Take water to your nose using the right hand, lightly sniff it in, and then quietly blow it out using the left hand while wiping the nose downward.

Number of times: x 3

Ruling: recommended

Face

Action: Take water into both hands to wash the entire face: from the hairline to the bottom of the chin, and from ear to ear. If you have a thick beard, use your fingers to comb the water through it.

Number of times: x 3

Ruling: first wash is <u>required.</u> 2nd and 3rd washes are recommended.

Arms

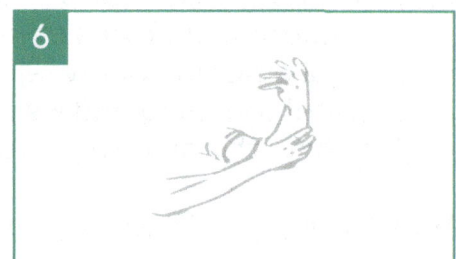

Action: Wash both arms from the fingertips up to and including the elbows. Start with the right arm then the left. Cup your palm and fill it with water then let the water flow down your arm while rubbing it.

Number of times: x 3 each side

Ruling: first wash of each arm is <u>required.</u> 2nd and 3rd washes are recommended.

Head	Ears	Feet
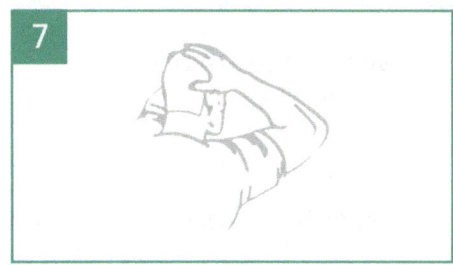	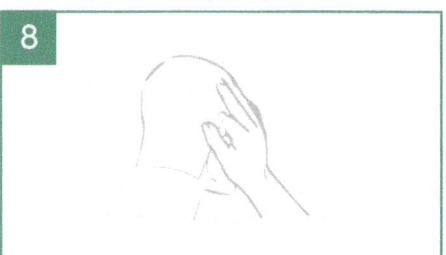	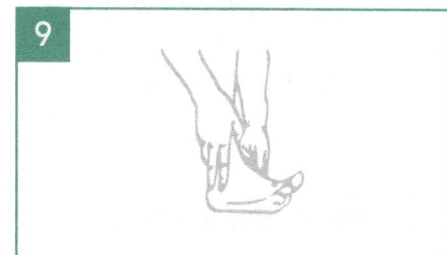

Action: Wet your hands, then wipe from the front of your head (where a normal hairline begins) to the top of the back of your neck.
→ If your hair is short or tied up, wipe back again in one motion.
→ If your hair is long, part your hair into two, and lay it on your chest. Wipe from scalp to tips.

Number of times: x 1

Ruling: required

Action: Re-wet the index fingers and thumbs and wipe the inside of the ears and the back of the earlobes.

Number of times: x 1

Ruling: recommended

Action: wash both feet, making sure to clean the entire foot from the tip of the toes (and between them), up to and including the ankles. Start with the right foot then the left.

Number of times: x 3 each side

Ruling: first wash of each foot is required. 2nd and 3rd washes are recommended.

End: After completing the wudu, it is recommended that one say the declaration of faith (shahada) to oneself as this was the practice of the Prophet Muhammad ﷺ.

Once you have done wudu, the wudu is valid until it's broken by either an act of minor or major ritual impurity. One wudu can be used for multiple prayers of the day as long as it hasn't been broken (by using the restroom, etc.)

Note: The above wudu combines both the required *(fard)* and recommended *(sunnah)* actions. You may find yourself in situations where you can only do the required actions. The required actions of wudu are to make an intention and wash:

- the entire face once,
- the arms from the fingertips up to and including the elbows once,
- wipe the head once, and
- wash the feet up to and including the ankles once.

Although this is the minimum requirement for wudu, doing the full wudu brings more blessings.

Circle the <u>required</u> actions of Wudu.

Making an intention	Saying "Bismillah"	Washing the hands to the wrists
Cleaning inside one's mouth	Cleaning inside one's nose	Washing the face
Washing the hands, arms, and elbows	Wiping the head	Wiping the ears
Washing the feet and ankles	Saying the Shahada at the end	

▦ **Prison Context**

Wudu should be performed in a place that does not offend others because wudu involves cleaning the mouth, nose, and feet, and sometimes leaves traces of dirt in these areas. Remember that it is an obligation to be respectful to your neighbor, and in prison, the entire prison population is your neighbor.

Additionally, the water should be hygienic: do not do wudu with toilet water.

2. Ghusl:

If the following below exist, then this person is in a state of major ritual impurity. This would require a major ritual showering (ghusl) before a person can pray. A person is only required to have ghusl for major ritual impurities.

1. Sexual intercourse (with or without ejaculation)
2. Ejaculation
3. The end of a menstrual period
4. The end of postpartum bleeding after childbirth
5. Death (the obligation falls on the Muslim community to perform ghusl for the deceased Muslim)

If a Muslim experiences any of the above, they would have to take a complete ritual shower (ghusl) to establish the state of purity necessary for prayer. In the case of menstruation and postpartum bleeding, women need to wait for these conditions to end before taking a complete shower to establish the state of purity.

How to Perform Ritual Showering (Ghusl)

Ghusl is done to end a state of major ritual impurity. To do ghusl:

2. Make the intention to purify yourself for worship,
3. Wash your private parts,
4. Make Wudu (ritual washing), and
5. Wash your entire body.

→ Make sure to rinse your mouth and nose since some scholars consider this obligatory.
→ Also make sure to wash every part of your body, especially the easy-to-miss places such as the ears, belly button, roots of the hair, back, buttocks and groin area, and between the toes. Remember to let water flow over all parts of the body.

🪟 Prison Context

There may be times when a person is in a state of major ritual impurity but cannot leave their cell to perform ghusl. In this case, they would perform ghusl by pouring water over their body with a cup, or even by squeezing water out of a soaked washcloth onto the body, allowing the water to completely run over each body part, and then wiping it. This would be acceptable and qualifies as ghusl.

When doing ghusl in this way, ensure to cover your private parts with a sheet or shorts and don't forget to clean up after yourself.

If there is no water in the cell, then one would be eligible to make **tayammum**.

Tayammum: What to Do When There Is No Water Available

In Allah's Wisdom and Generosity, He has provided a way for Muslims to worship Him even if they have no access to clean water.

This mode of preparation for prayer is called dry ritual purification (tayammum). It involves using clean earth or unprocessed stone to wipe the face and the arms.

This method of purification can be used whether a person needs to perform ritual washing (wudu) or ritual showering (ghusl) when water is not available. Allah says in the Quran:

> **❴ If you are sick, or in travel, or if one of you has come after relieving himself, or you have had contact with women, and cannot find water, then purify yourselves with clean earth, wiping your faces and hands. ❵**
> **Quran 4:43**

Tayammum can also be used in the following situations:

- Water is available but is at least one mile away
- Water is available at a very high price
- A person has water enough for cooking and drinking but not enough for wudu
- Using water would cause a person to become sick or would worsen a medical condition. This includes wounds, stitches and casts.

How to Perform Dry Ritual Purification (Tayammum)

Tayammum involves 4 steps:

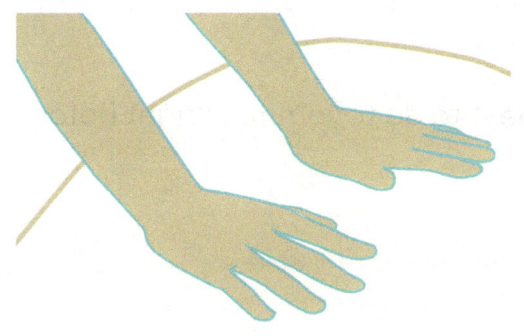

1 Make the intention to pray and then find clean dry soil, earth or unprocessed stone. Place both hands upon it, palms down, then shake off the excess dust that accumulates on the hands.

2 Wipe the entire face in the same manner as in wudu, but only one time.

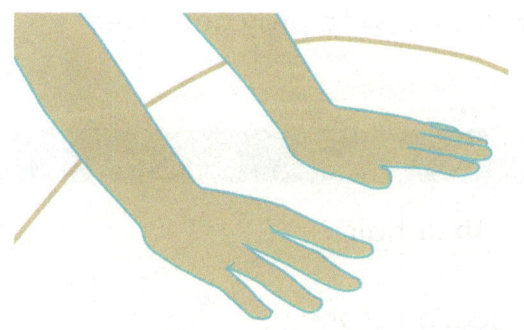

3 Again, place both hands upon some clean dry soil/earth/unprocessed stone, palms down, and again shake off the excess dust.

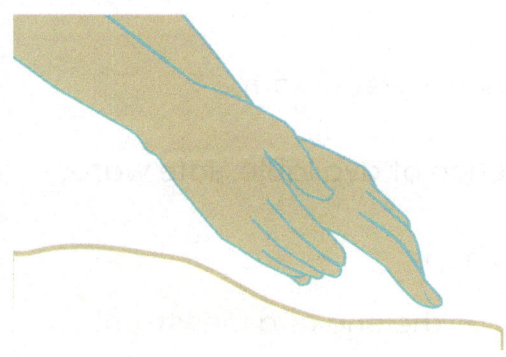

4 Lastly, wipe each entire hand and arm from the fingertips up to and including the elbow in the same manner as if washing them one time. Start with wiping the right arm. Then finish with the left. Don't forget to wipe between the fingers.

What Invalidates Tayammum?

1. Tayammum is invalidated by all the things that invalidate wudu or require ghusl (sleeping, urination, passing wind, etc.).

2. If a person finds water after having completed tayammum, he or she must perform the regular wudu/ghusl since tayammum now becomes invalid.

3. One must do tayammum for each obligatory prayer. It is best to do tayammum right before the prayer.

Prison Context

It may be that a prisoner will not be able to get to water during one of the prayer times due to an emergency like a lockdown or restricted movement. In these cases, if one believes that the prayer time will end before they get water, then they must do tayammum to pray. It may be wise to keep a small bag of soil in your living quarters in case of this type of emergency. Make sure that you are not breaking any institutional rules by doing this.

3. **Inward Preparation:** Preparing our hearts and minds

Before we pray, we should try to free our hearts and minds from anything other than Allah and His beloved Messenger ﷺ. Know that you are addressing Allah when you pray, and following the lead of His Messenger ﷺ who showed us how to pray and loves the prayer.

Fill in the blank. Write: wudu, ghusl, or tayammum.

_____ : this requires a person to wash their hair

_____ : this is done with soil or unprocessed stone

_____ : this requires one to wash their face, arms, wipe their heads, and wash their feet

_____ : one needs to do this after having a wet dream

_____ : this is invalidated by the presence of available, safe water

_____ : this is invalidated by falling asleep

_____ : women are required to do this at the end of a menstrual period

Preparing for Prayer and Bleeding

Women may experience bleeding for different reasons such as:

1. Menstruation (a period)
2. Post-Natal Bleeding
3. Mid-Cycle Bleeding (for any reason)

While a woman is menstruating or experiencing post-natal bleeding, the obligation for prayer is lifted. In fact, it is forbidden for women to pray the five daily prayers during these times. Women do not make up the missed prayers afterwards. During these times, women also do not perform wudu, ghusl, or tayammum. Once these conditions end, a woman performs ghusl and resumes praying.

In addition to not praying, a woman experiencing these conditions also does not:

⊘ Fast: unfasted days in Ramadan are made up. See Chapter 6

⊘ Stay in a masjid: prison chapels are not masjids. Women can still attend events held in these spaces when menstruating.

⊘ Pass through a masjid: this is only if a woman is afraid of soiling the masjid.

⊘ Perform certain parts of pilgrimage: These will be covered in future texts as they require traveling to Makkah.

⊘ Engage in sexual pleasure between the navel (belly button) and knees.

⊘ Get divorced.

In Islam, menstruating and post-natal bleeding are not a punishment. In fact, Allah has commanded the believing women to avoid certain actions, and by following the commands of Allah, women are in a state of obedience and worship to Allah.

→ The maximum length of menstruation per month: Islamically, the maximum number of days for menstruation is 15 days. A woman must perform ghusl at the end of menstruation (or after 15 days of bleeding) and resume prayer.

→ The minimum length of time between two menstruation cycles: The minimum length of time between two menstrual cycles is 15 consecutive days without seeing blood. If a woman sees blood before 15 days are up, she must continue to pray.

→ The maximum length of post-natal bleeding: Islamically, the maximum number of days for post-natal bleeding is 60 days. A woman must perform ghusl at the end of post-natal bleeding (or after 60 days of bleeding) and resume prayer.

Mid-cycle Bleeding:

A woman that continues to bleed after 15 days of menstruation, or 60 days of post-natal bleeding is required to wash away the blood, change sanitary items with blood, and do wudu for every prayer for the duration of the bleeding.

There are no restrictions for a woman that is experiencing mid-cycle bleeding. She may fast, go to the masjid, and do all the other actions a menstruating woman cannot do.

Periods and bleeding aren't always straightforward, and every woman's situation is unique. If you have questions about when to pray, please reach out to your Tayba Foundation coach or instructor.

Preparation for Prayer (Salah)

Write 3 things one can do to prepare for prayer.

1

2

3

List 2 differences between wudu and ghusl.

Circle True or False.

1	One can do tayammum if water is too expensive.	**True / False**
2	One wipes their feet with soil in tayammum.	**True / False**
3	Wudu is often done multiple times a day.	**True / False**
4	Falling asleep invalidates tayammum.	**True / False**
5	Tayammum done to replace wudu or ghusl is done in the same way for both.	**True / False**
6	If you don't have enough water for ghusl, make wudu instead.	**True / False**

What is the main purpose of prayer?

Preparation for Prayer (Salah)

How does purifying yourself before prayer help you prepare?

Did you learn anything in this chapter that surprised you?

What are some of the most important things you learned/reviewed in this chapter?

This is an optional section.
Completing it is not necessary for the successful completion of this book.

Masjids Around the World – Art Therapy

Copy/draw, decorate or color this masjid while learning about it.

Al Masjid an Nabawi (The Prophet's Masjid), Madinah

The Messenger of Allah, Prophet Muhammad ﷺ migrated to Madinah from Makkah. There, the Muslims grew in number and strength. The Prophet ﷺ is buried in his masjid, under the green dome. Al Masjid an Nabawi is one of the holiest sites in Islam. Another name for Madinah is Tayba. That's where Tayba Foundation gets its name.

Art by: Henry Fuller, Tayba student

Performing Prayer (Salah)

MAIN POINTS

- One must be dressed properly for prayer by covering one's nakedness.
- Muslims face the Ka'ba when performing the five required prayers.
- There are five required daily prayers, each with a specific time period and number of cycles.
- There is a specific prescribed way to perform the required prayers.
- Praying with others has a very large reward.

LEARNING OBJECTIVES

- To understand and implement the preconditions of performing prayer
- To demonstrate the steps of performing prayer

Reflection Questions

- How does prayer play a large role in your life?
- What motivates you to keep praying?

Key Terms

- **Ka'ba:** the cubic house of worship built by Prophets Ibrahim and Ismail in Makkah
- **Qibla:** the direction of prayer
- **Fajr:** morning prayer before sunrise
- **Dhuhr:** midday prayer
- **Asr:** late afternoon prayer
- **Maghrib:** sunset prayer
- **'Isha:** Night prayer
- **Adhan:** Call to prayer
- **Iqama:** Call to rise to prayer

Standing For Prayer

Once you have:

1. Removed all filth from your body, clothes, and place of prayer,
2. Are in a state of ritual purity (wudu, ghusl, or tayammum),
3. Have dressed properly for prayer,
4. Are facing the approximate direction of the Ka'ba, and
5. Have certainty that the prayer time has begun,

You have done all things required to do before starting the prayer.

We have already discussed numbers 1 and 2 in Chapter 3, so let's proceed to numbers 3, 4, and 5.

3. Dress for Prayer

Being dressed properly for prayer means at least having one's nakedness covered. Due to differences in the creation of the male and female, the Islamic definition of nakedness is different.

For men, the minimum that must be covered in order for prayer to be valid is from the navel (bellybutton) to the knees. However it is better for men to cover their shoulders, chest, and stomachs (such as wearing a shirt).

For women, the nakedness includes the entire body except for the hands, face, and soles of the feet. Some scholars allow all of the feet to be shown.

4. Face the Qibla

‹ Wherever you are ˹O Prophet˺, turn your face towards the Sacred Mosque.
And wherever you ˹believers˺ are, face towards it ›
Quran 2:150

The Ka'ba is a house of worship built in Makkah originally by Prophets Abraham (Ibrahim) and his son Ishmael (Ismail) purely for the worship of Allah. To face the Ka'ba means to find its direction (meaning the direction of Makkah) wherever you are and to face that direction while performing salah. This direction of prayer is called **_qibla_**.

In the USA many communities pray northeast, while some pray southeast, both have valid positions. Therefore, if it becomes difficult for you to find the direction, then look to see what direction the sun rises in the morning and establish the direction of the east. Then at least you have some point of direction until you have a better understanding of the difference of opinions.

If there is no way of finding out which way the qilba is, try to make an educated guess.

How did you first figure out the qibla for your prayer?

5. Making sure the Prayer time has Begun

Prayer Times And Number of Cycles

Each of the five prayers has a specified time to be prayed and a specified number of required cycles (explained later). Before praying, a person must ensure that the prayer time has begun. These are the prayer times:

1.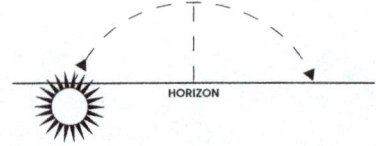

   Fajr (morning prayer)
   From dawn (once light appears on the horizon) up until sunrise.

   Length: 2 cycles

2.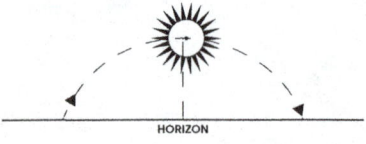

   Dhuhr (midday prayer)
   Once the sun passes its zenith (highest point in the sky) up until an object's shadow is equal in length to its height.

   Length: 4 cycles

3.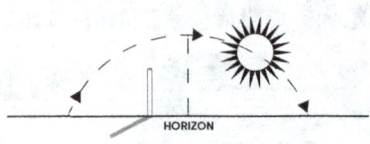

   'Asr (late afternoon prayer)
   Once an object casts a shadow (from the sun) that is equal to its height, up until the sun has completely set.

   Length: 4 cycles

4.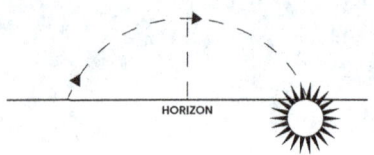

   Maghrib (sunset prayer)
   Once the sun sets, up until the light is fully gone from the sky. This might not be visible from prison and you may need to rely on a prayer-time calendar.

   Length: 3 cycles

5.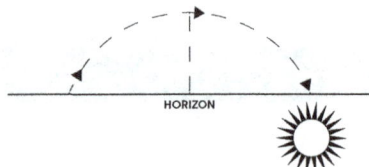

   'Isha (night prayer)
   After the last pinks of sunset fade and the sky turns fully dark until dawn (Fajr prayer).

   Length: 4 cycles

It is permissible to pray at any time between the beginning of the prayer and its end. Some people incorrectly think that you have to pray as soon as the prayer starts or you are being sinful. That is not true. Praying at the beginning of the prayer's time is highly recommended, but so is delaying the prayer if it will allow more people to attend.

Many Muslims use prayer charts and cellphone apps to know when each prayer time has begun. These methods are calculations based on the movements of the sun mentioned above. It's best to wait a few minutes after the prayer time begins so that you can pray.

What do you use to tell the time for prayer?

The Call to Prayer (Adhan) and the Call to Rise (Iqama)

Call to Prayer (adhan)

ARABIC PRONUNCIATION	MEANING IN ENGLISH	RECITE
ALLAHU AKBAR!	ALLAH IS GREATER!	4X
ASHHADU AN LAA E-LAHA IL-LA-LAH!	I BEAR WITNESS THAT THERE IS NO DEITY, EXCEPT ALLAH!	2X
ASH HADU ANNA MUHAMMADUR RASOOLILAH!	I BEAR WITNESS THAT MUHAMMAD IS THE MESSENGER OF ALLAH!	2X
HAYYA ALAS SALAH!	COME TO PRAYER!	2X
HAYYA ALAL FALAH!	COME TO SUCCESS!	2X
ALLAHU AKBAR!	ALLAH IS GREATER!	2X
LAA ELAHA ILLA LAH!	THERE IS NO DEITY BUT ALLAH!	1X

In Muslim countries and in many mosques, the notification to Muslims that the prayer time has entered is by means of the Call to Prayer *(adhan)*. It is usually chanted in a rhythmic fashion and consists of phrases that are repeated one after another. But it should not be sung.

After this call to prayer, Muslims often do wudu and other necessary preparations for prayer.

Call to Rise for Prayer (iqama)

ARABIC PRONUNCIATION	MEANING IN ENGLISH	RECITE
ALLAHU AKBAR!	ALLAH IS GREATER!	2X
ASHHADU AN LAA E-LAHA IL-LA-LAH!	I BEAR WITNESS THAT THERE IS NO DEITY, EXCEPT ALLAH!	1X
ASH HADU ANNA MUHAMMADUR RASOOLILAH!	I BEAR WITNESS THAT MUHAMMAD IS THE MESSENGER OF ALLAH!	1X
HAYYA ALAS SALAH!	COME TO PRAYER!	1X
HAYYA ALAL FALAH!	COME TO SUCCESS!	1X
QAD QAAMAH TUS-SALAH!	RISE FOR PRAYER!	2X
ALLAHU AKBAR!	ALLAH IS GREATER!	2X
LAA ELAHA ILLA LAH!	THERE IS NO DEITY BUT ALLAH!	1X

Once the prayer is about to begin, usually the same person who called the call to prayer (adhan) stands and calls the "rise to prayer" *(iqama)* which signals everyone to line up shoulder to shoulder because the prayer is starting. This call to rise for prayer (iqama) is usually recited much faster and without much rhythm.

How to Pray

1 ## Intention

Begin with your intention. Clear your heart of all worldly matters and feelings. Focus on your goal, which is to worship Allah who deserves to be worshiped. Then, in your heart, intend to pray whichever prayer you stood for.

2 ## Takbeer

Begin your prayer by raising your hands, with the palms open and facing forward, up to your shoulders, and declare His Greatness by saying the takbeer: **"Allahu Akbar!"** (Allah is the Greatest)

3 ## Standing

At the same time, place your right hand over your left hand on your body below the chest and above the navel. This is the standing position. (Imam Malik also allowed leaving the arms down at the sides. Both positions are acceptable.)

While Standing

1st: Recite the opening chapter of the Quran, Surah Al-Fatiha (1:1-7):

"Alhamdu lillaahi rabbil 'alameen,
Ar Rahmaanir-Raheem,
Maaliki yawmid-deen,
Iyyaaka na'budu, wa iyyaaka nasta'een,
Ihdinas-siraat al mustaqeem;
Siraatal-ladhina an 'amta 'alayhim,
Ghayril maghdoobi 'alayhim walad-daaleen." Ameen

2nd: Then proceed on to reciting a short chapter (surah) from the Qur'an (like chapter 112, Surah Al-Ikhlas)

"Qul huwal-Laahu ahad,
Allahus-samad, lam yalid wa lam yoolad
Wa lam yakul-lahu kufu-wan ahad."

Look up the meanings of these chapters in your copy of the Quran.

4 Bowing

Then say **Allahu Akbar** (Allah is the Greatest) while standing and move to the next position: bowing.

With your hands on your knees say: "**Subhana rabbiyal adheem**" (3 times) which means, "How glorious is my Lord, the Majestic!"

(Note: Saying this one time is acceptable but more is better.)

5 Brief Standing

While moving back to the standing position, say "**Sami Allahu li-man hamida**," which means, "Allah heard the one who praised Him."

Once completely standing again, say: "**Rabbana wa lakal hamd**" which means, "Our Lord! For You is all praise!"

(Note: If you are praying behind an imam (prayer leader), the imam would say "Sami Allahu li-man hamida" and you would only say "Rabbana wa lakal hamd.")

First Prostration

6

Then say, "**Allahu Akbar**" (Allah is the Greatest) and move toward the next position, which is called prostration. In prostration, your nose and forehead, as well as your hands, should touch the ground while your elbows should not touch the ground.

While in this position, say: "Subhana Rabbiyal a'la" (3 times) which means, "How glorious is my Lord, the Most High!"

(Note: Saying this one time is acceptable but more is better.)

While in prostration, you can make dua (calling on Allah) in any language. The Prophet  said that, "The servant is closest to his Lord during prostration, so increase your supplications therein." (Sahih Muslim) Use prostration as an opportunity to ask Allah for whatever you want.

7 Brief Sitting

Then say, "**Allahu Akbar**" (Allah is the Greatest) while at the same time rising up to the sitting position. Your hands should be resting on your thighs.

8 Second Prostration

Then say, "**Allahu Akbar**" (Allah is the Greatest) while moving back into the prostration position. Again, say "**Subhana Rabbiyal a'la**" (3 times).

You have just completed one cycle of prayer.

9 Second Cycle

While saying Allahu Akbar, return back to the standing position, and repeat steps 3-8.

10 Prayer of Greetings upon the Prophet ﷺ

At the end of the second cycle, after performing the two prostrations as described in steps 6-8, move to the sitting position. While holding the right hand in a fist with the index finger pointing toward the direction of prayer (qibla), recite the prayer of greetings upon the Prophet Muhammad ﷺ:

"**At-tahiyyatu lillahi, was-salawatu, wat-tayyibatu. Assalamu 'alayka ayyuhan nabeeyu wa rahmatullahi wa barakatuh. Assalamu 'alayna wa 'ala 'ibaadil-lahis saliheen. Ash-hadu an la ilaha illAllah, wa ash-hada anna Muhammadan 'abduhu wa rasoolooh.**"

Meaning: "All greetings of authority are for Allah, along with prayers and all good deeds. Peace be upon you, O Prophet, along with the mercy of Allah and His blessings!

Peace be upon us, and upon all of the righteous Servants of Allah. I bear witness that there is nothing worthy of worship except Allah, and I bear witness that Muhammad ﷺ is His servant and messenger."

11 Last Seating of Prayer: The Abrahamic Greeting

If a person is on the last cycle, and seated at the end of their prayer, he or she would then say the Abrahamic Greeting after the prayer of greetings (step 10):

"Allahumma salli 'ala Muhammadin wa 'ala 'ali Muhammadin, kama sallayta 'ala Ibraheema wa 'ala 'ali Ibraaheem. Wa barik 'ala Muhammadin wa 'ala 'ali Muhammad, kama barakta 'ala Ibraheema wa 'ala 'ali Ibraheem, innaka hamidum majeed!"

Meaning: "O Allah! Send your salutations upon Muhammad and upon the family of Muhammad, in the same manner that you sent salutations upon Abraham and upon the family of Abraham. And bless Muhammad, and the family of Muhammad, in the same manner that you blessed Abraham and the Family of Abraham; surely You are Praiseworthy, Exalted!"

> **2-cycle Prayer**
> - Steps 1-12

12 Ending Salutations

At this point a person is ready to end his or her prayer. He or she does that by turning the head to the right shoulder and saying the salutation which is: **"As-salaamu 'alaykum wa rahmatullaah"** (may the peace and mercy of Allah be upon you). Then turn the head to the left shoulder while saying the same.

All prayers consist of two, three or four cycles. The above is a description of a prayer that only consists of two cycles (such as the Fajr prayer). What follows is a description of a three and then a four cycle prayer.

Three cycles (Maghrib prayer):

1. After performing steps 1 through 10 as listed above, say Allahu Akbar and immediately get up into the standing position.
2. Then recite only the Opening chapter of the Quran (Al-Fatiha) without any other recitation (first part of step 3).
3. Then complete the prayer as described in steps 4 through 12.

> **3-cycle Prayer**
> - Steps 1-10
> - Steps 3-8
> - Steps 10-12

Four cycles (Dhuhr, Asr, Isha prayers):

1. After performing two cycles by following steps 1 through 10 as listed above, say Allahu Akbar and immediately get up into the standing position.
2. Then recite only the opening chapter (Surah Al-Fatiha) without any other recitation, then complete the bowing and prostrations as described in steps 3 through 8.
3. Stand again for the 4th cycle, recite Surah Al-Fatiha without any other recitation and then complete the prayer as described in steps 3 through 12.

> **4-cycle Prayer**
> - Steps 1-10
> - Steps 3-8
> - Steps 3-12

Note: This description on how to perform prayer covers the required parts. For the sake of ease, not all recommended parts are covered, as this is an introductory course.

Additionally – Some scholars mention a few recommended differences in how men and women pray, like arm position while standing. But since the required actions of prayer are the same, these details aren't included in this book.

Pray a two-cycle prayer following all the steps mentioned above. Try to commit the Arabic texts to memory.

Things Which Invalidate the Prayer

It is of utmost importance that one maintains concentration on prayer and the focus of prayer: Allah. There are actions that can invalidate the prayer. The prayer would then need to be redone.

These things include:

🚫 Speaking out loud with words that are not part of the prayer, whether intentional or not

🚫 Moving excessively in the prayer (multiple unnecessary actions that are not part of the prayer itself)

🚫 Eating or drinking during prayer

🚫 Turning one's body completely away from the direction of prayer (qibla)

🚫 Laughing out loud in the prayer

Prayer: A Guide

Tear out this page if needed and use it as a guide when praying.

2 - Cycle Prayer

First cycle:

 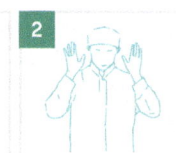      

| | Say: Allahu Akbar (to begin prayer) | Recite Fatihah and another short chapter | | | | | |

Second cycle:

  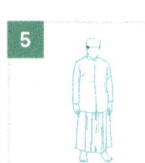    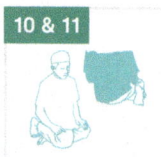 

Recite Fatihah and another short chapter

10 & 11 Recite the Prayer of Greetings upon the Prophet ﷺ and The Abrahamic Greeting.

12 Say the ending salutation (to end the prayer)

3 - Cycle Prayer

First cycle:

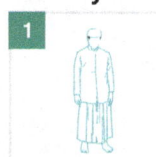  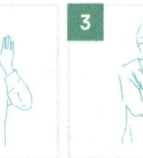   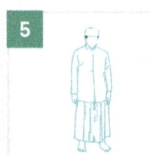   

| | Say: Allahu Akbar (to begin prayer) | Recite Fatihah and another short chapter | | | | | |

Second cycle:

  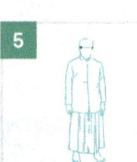    

Recite Fatihah and another short chapter

10 Recite the Prayer of Greetings upon the Prophet ﷺ only

Third cycle:

   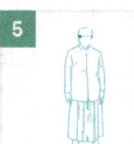     

Recite Fatihah only

10 & 11 Recite the Prayer of Greetings upon the Prophet ﷺ and The Abrahamic Greeting.

12 Say the ending salutation (to end the prayer)

4 - Cycle Prayer

First cycle:

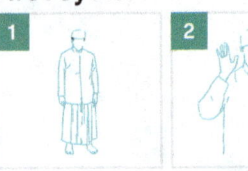       

Say: Allahu Akbar (to begin prayer)

Recite Fatihah and another short chapter

Second cycle:

Recite Fatihah and another short chapter

Recite the Prayer of Greetings upon the Prophet ﷺ only

Third cycle:

Recite Fatihah only

Fourth cycle:

   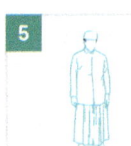     

Recite Fatihah only

Recite the Prayer of Greetings upon the Prophet ﷺ and The Abrahamic Greeting.

Say the ending salutation (to end the prayer)

Al Fatiha

"Alhamdu lillaahi rabbil 'alameen, Ar Rahmaanir-Raheem, Maaliki yawmid-deen, Iyyaaka na'budu, wa iyyaaka nasta'een, Ihdinas-siraat al mustaqeem; Siraatal-ladhina an 'amta 'alayhim, Ghayril maghdoobi 'alayhim walad-daaleen."

Prayer of Greeting upon the Prophet ﷺ

"At-tahiyyatu lillahi, was-salawatu, wat-tayyibatu. Assalamu 'alayka ayyuhan nabeeyu wa rahmatullahi wa barakatuh. Assalamu 'alayna wa 'ala 'ibaadil-lahis saliheen. Ash-hadu an la ilaha illAllah, wa ash-hada anna Muhammadan 'abduhu wa rasoolooh."

The Abrahamic Greeting

"Allahumma salli 'ala Muhammadin wa 'ala 'ali Muhammadin, kama sallayta 'ala Ibraheema wa 'ala 'ali Ibraaheem. Wa barik 'ala Muhammadin wa 'ala 'ali Muhammad, kama barakta 'ala Ibraheema wa 'ala 'ali Ibraheem, innaka hamidum majeed!"

Group/Congregational Prayer

When two or more people pray together, whether it is in a masjid or elsewhere, it is considered congregational prayer. Congregational prayer is one of the most emphasized Prophetic Practices (sunnah). This is due to the many statements of the Messenger of Allah ﷺ which describe the virtues and rewards of congregational prayer:

"A man's prayer with one other man is better than his praying alone, and a man's prayer with two other men is better than his praying with one other. The more there are, the more beloved that is to Allah."
(Sahih Abu Dawud)

Leading the Prayer

When there is no designated <u>imam</u> (prayer leader), the congregational prayer is led by the most qualified person. This means the one who:

1. Has the most knowledge of prayer
2. Has memorized the most Qur'an
3. Is morally upright
4. Is accepted by the people

The Imam should recite the Quran verses out loud in the first two cycles of the prayers: Fajr, Maghrib, and Isha.

Be careful never to move before the imam in prayer, such as starting to bow or going into prostration before the imam does.

Performing Prayer (Salah)

Fill in the table.

Prayer	Time of Day	Number of Cycles
Fajr		
	Midday	
		4
Maghrib		
		4

Write the correct word.

_____ : This chapter of the Quran is recited in every cycle.

_____ : Do this action twice in each cycle. Sit in between both.

_____ : Make your intention then say this to begin your prayer.

_____ : This greeting is only read in the final seating of prayer.

Write two of each.

Things you need to do before prayer to prepare for it:

1

2

Things that invalidate the prayer:

1

2

Performing Prayer (Salah)

How does praying in congregation contribute to a sense of unity among the Muslims?

What you learned in this chapter is how to pray as taught by the Prophet ﷺ and as Muslims have prayed for many centuries all over the world. How does this make you feel?

What are some of the most important things you learned/reviewed in this chapter?

This is an optional section.
Completing it is not necessary for the successful completion of this book.

Masjids Around the World – Art Therapy

Copy/draw, decorate or color this masjid while learning about it.

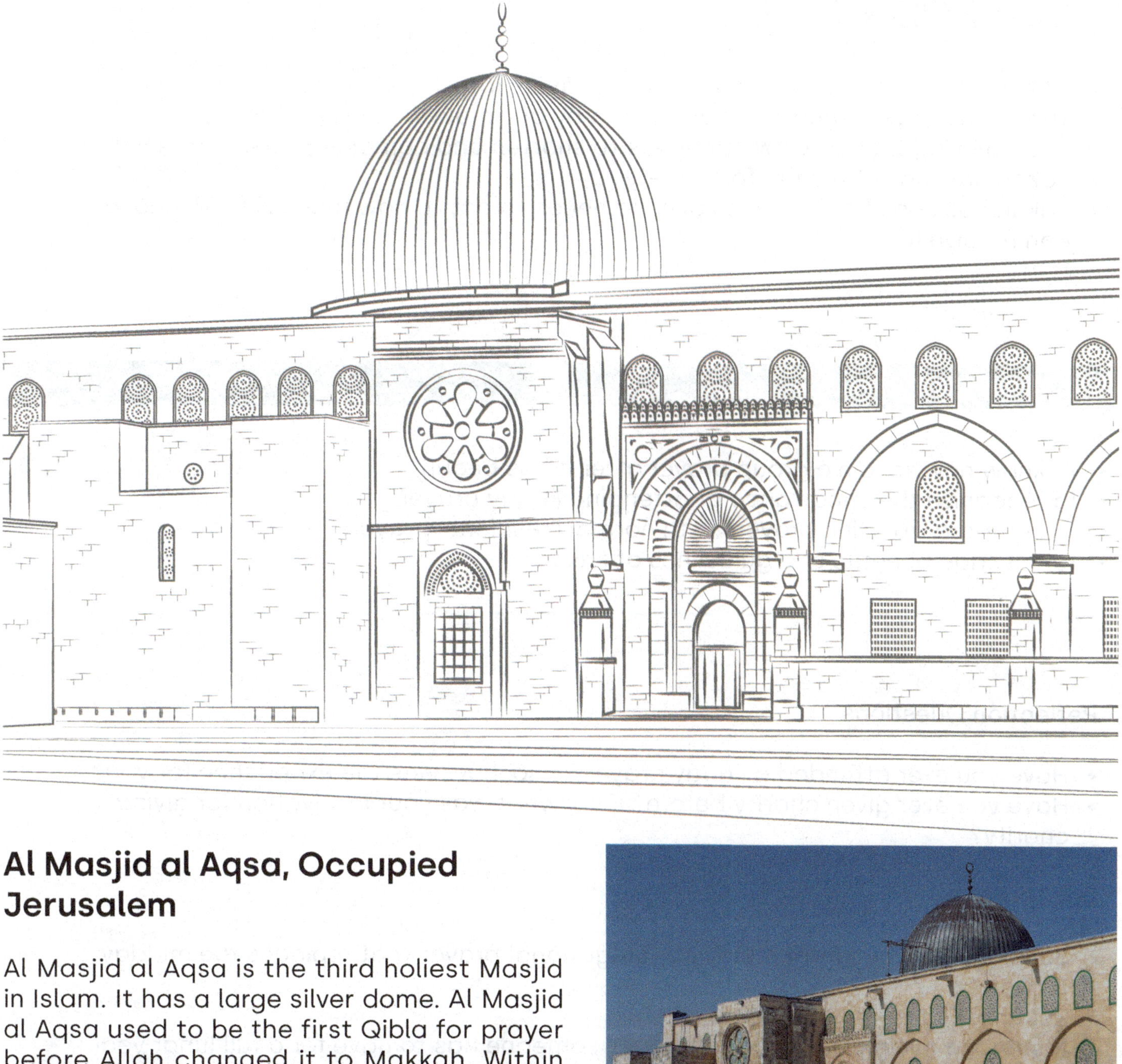

Al Masjid al Aqsa, Occupied Jerusalem

Al Masjid al Aqsa is the third holiest Masjid in Islam. It has a large silver dome. Al Masjid al Aqsa used to be the first Qibla for prayer before Allah changed it to Makkah. Within it, the Prophet Muhammad ﷺ led the other Prophets in congregation prayer on the Night of Ascention (Al Isra' wal Mi'raj). On this night, the honor of the five obligatory prayers was revealed to the Muslims.

Other Prayer Topics + Zakah

MAIN POINTS

- One is allowed to join congregational prayers late.
- The Friday prayer should not be missed by any male who can attend it.
- The traveling prayer allows travelers to shorten and combine prayers for ease.
- Zakah has many benefits for society.
- Zakah has specific guidelines on who needs to pay it, how much is paid, and who can receive it.

LEARNING OBJECTIVES

- To know how to join a group prayer after it has begun
- To recognize the importance of attending Friday prayer
- To compare traveling prayers with normal (resident) prayers
- To describe benefits and guidelines of zakah

Reflection Questions

- Have you ever attended a Friday prayer? If so, how was the experience for you?
- Have you ever given charity before? If so, what was your motivation for giving charity?

Key Terms

- **Jumuah:** the obligatory Friday congregational prayer that replaces the midday prayer
- **Zakah:** obligatory alms
- **Nisab:** the minimum amount of money someone has to have for a full lunar year before paying zakah

Joining the Prayer Late

As mentioned in the last chapter, praying with others brings more reward than praying alone.

If you come to the group prayer late, join the group in the position they are in.

1. Say "Allahu Akbar" **while standing** to start praying.
2. Then join whatever position the group is in (steps 3 onwards) and follow the imam in whatever he does afterwards. Do not wait for the imam to move onto another action.
3. Once the imam ends the prayer with the ending salutation (step 12), you simply stand up and complete the number of cycles you have missed.

You missed the cycle if you joined the prayer *after* the bowing position (Step 5 onwards). If you join the prayer before or during the bowing position (Steps 2-4), you do not make up that cycle.

Scenario 1:
A person arrives late to the group prayer while the imam and followers are in the bowing position:

1. The person says "Allahu Akbar" while standing.

2. The person immediately joins the bowing position with everyone else.

Because this person has caught the bowing position in the first cycle, this person is not considered as having missed any part of the prayer.

⊘ Outcome: Finish the prayer with everyone else.

Scenario 2:
A person arrives late to a group prayer while the imam and followers are in the prostration position:

1. The person says "Allahu Akbar" while standing.

2. The person immediately joins the prostration position with everyone else.

Because this person caught the cycle after the bowing ended (step 5 onwards), this person missed this cycle.

⟳ Outcome: As soon as the Imam ends the prayer, stand up and complete the missing cycles (go back to step 3 onwards for what you missed). Do <u>not</u> follow the Imam in the ending salutations (step 12).

The Friday Prayer (Jumuah)

The Friday prayer is an obligatory gathering to pray of all the resident Muslim men in a particular area once a week, in one predesignated location.

Jumuah prayer replaces the midday prayer (Dhuhr) on Fridays. It consists of only two cycles. Two short sermons are given before these two cycles. This prayer has many rewards and should not be missed by anyone who can attend. Allah says in the Qur'an:

⟨**O believers! When the call to prayer is made on Friday, then proceed ˹diligently˺ to the remembrance of Allah and leave off ˹your˺ business. That is best for you, if only you knew.**⟩
Quran 62:9

Very large crowds show up for Jummah prayer in countries with large Muslim populations.

Also, the Messenger of Allah ﷺ said, "Friday is the best day on which the sun rises. On this day, Adam was created; on it he was admitted into Paradise, and on it he was turned out of it. The Day of Judgment will also take place on Friday." (Sahih Muslim)

<u>When attending the Friday Prayer:</u>

- It is required to remain silent during the sermons. Listening attentively is considered an act of worship.
- It is highly recommended for those attending Friday Prayer to clean themselves of all bodily odors by bathing, brushing their teeth, wearing freshly cleaned clothes and some type of perfume.
- It is not required for women, children, the sick, the handicapped, or travelers to attend the Friday Prayer. They pray the midday (Dhuhr) prayer instead.
- If someone misses Friday prayer (or is unable to attend one in prison) they must pray the midday prayer (Dhuhr) instead. In prison, if Muslims are unable to arrange Jumuah together, the obligation is lifted.
- Eating, drinking, fidgeting, and inattentiveness are highly disliked during the sermon.

What was the sermon about at the last Jumuah you attended?

Prayer of the Traveler

One of the great mercies of Allah is His permission to lighten obligations whenever there are hardships.

Because traveling can be a hardship, Muslims are allowed to shorten their prayers if traveling at least 51 miles away from the edge of their city limits. The traveler's prayer is done both during traveling and at a temporary destination.

The traveler's prayer has three aspects: 1) Shortening prayers, 2) Combining prayers, 3) Arriving at the destination.

1. Shortening prayers: Four cycle prayers are prayed as two cycle prayers. Two and three cycle prayers are always prayed the same length.
2. Combining prayers in one prayer time: A traveler may also pray two prayers in one prayer time.

   → Midday (Dhuhr) prayer and late afternoon prayer (Asr): can be prayed at the time of either prayer
   → Sunset (Maghrib) prayer and night ('Isha) prayer: can be prayed at the time of either prayer.
   → Dawn (Fajr) prayer is not combined with any other prayer.

A person is traveling on a bus from 9pm to 2am. There will be no time to stop for sunset prayer. They are staying at that transfer center for two full days. Once the person stops for the night, the person should:

» Pray the sunset (Maghrib) prayer as 3 cycles then
» Pray the night (Isha) prayer as 2 cycles

3. Arriving at the destination: Once the traveler reaches their destination, if one plans to stay at the destination for more than four days (excluding the day of arrival and the day of departure), one must pray the regular number of cycles.

A person is traveling on a bus from 9pm to 2am. There will be no time to stop for sunset prayer. They arrive at the transfer center and will be staying there for a week. Once the person stops for the night, the person should:

» Pray the sunset (Maghrib) prayer as 3 cycles then
» Pray the night (Isha) prayer as 4 cycles

Answer these questions on your own then compare your answers to the answers at the end of the chapter: page 62.

1 A person is being transferred to a new facility 120 miles away for the next few years of their sentence. The bus will not stop for the midday (dhuhr) prayer. It will be the afternoon (asr) prayer by the time the person arrives. What does the person do? Why?

2 It is time for the midday (dhuhr) prayer. A person will begin traveling at 3pm. How does one pray the midday (dhuhr) prayer before travel? Can they join it with the afternoon (asr) prayer?

3 A person arrives at a transfer facility at 5am after traveling for 10 hours. It is time for the dawn (fajr) prayer. They will leave the same day to another facility. How does this person pray the dawn (fajr) prayer? Why?

The Third Pillar of Islam: Obligatory Alms (Zakah)

❴...Establish prayer and give zakah and loan to Allah a goodly loan. And whatever good you put forward for yourselves—you will find it with Allah. It is better and greater in reward...❵
Quran 73:20

Paying the obligatory alms *(zakah)* is the third pillar of Islam. This is the way for the wealthy believers to take care of the needy believers.

<u>Paying Zakah has many benefits:</u>

- It helps to purify the heart from selfishness and greed.
- It is a way of showing gratefulness to Allah for what He has given you.
- It is an expression of true community where the giver is taking care of the less fortunate, and those less fortunate feel grateful and supported instead of envious of the wealthy.
- It is a way of circulating the wealth of a society to all of its members instead of it being concentrated in the pockets of a few.
- It purifies the person's wealth from anything that may have come to it unlawfully without their knowledge.

<u>Who Pays Zakah?</u>

Every Muslim who has the monetary equivalent of 3 ounces of gold (today about $6,800) in their possession for at least one lunar year (355 days) is required to pay zakah. This is known as the minimum amount *(nisab)* at which a person becomes responsible for paying Zakah. This person must give 2.5% of their saved wealth.

A person with $10,000 in savings only needs to give $250 for Zakah!

<u>Prison Context</u>

Unless someone has about $6,800 in savings, they are not required to pay zakah and are more likely to be its recipient. It's highly unlikely that anyone in prison would be required to pay zakah unless they happened to have personal savings which haven't been exhausted by legal fees.

Restorative justice is a branch of repentance. Repentance in Islam necessitates that any stolen/unlawfully acquired wealth be returned or removed from one's possession. So if someone had become incarcerated for property crimes like forged checks, embezzled funds, or stolen merchandise and still had the wealth or merchandise in their possession, any money acquired through those means belongs to the people it was taken from and must be returned. If that is not possible, then it must be donated to a legitimate charitable organization. This is even if these crimes were committed prior to becoming Muslim. Becoming Muslim wipes away past sins, but it doesn't cancel out other people's rights.

<u>Other Types of Charity</u>

Charity has a very special place in Islam, and all Muslims are encouraged to be as charitable as they can be. This charity can be given in large or small amounts.

There is a special obligatory alm called Zakat-al-Fitr given after the month of Ramadan during Eid al-Fitr. Though it is a type of zakah, it is different from the yearly zakah mentioned here.

Answers from questions on page 60

1. This person will combine the midday (dhuhr) prayer and afternoon (asr) prayer but will not shorten either one. Both are 4 cycles each. The reason is that: the first prayer time entered while the person was traveling so the person could have combined or shortened at that time. However, since they arrived and are no longer traveling, the person can no longer use the exceptions unique to travelers. So prayers are prayed at their full length.

2. Before travel, a person prays the full length of the prayer. The travel did not begin yet – so this prayer cannot be combined with any other.

3. The dawn (Fajr) prayer is always 2 cycles. Traveling doesn't change that.

Other Prayer Topics + Zakah

Circle the correct answer.

When you join the prayer late and the congregation is in the bowing position:

a. You start your prayer with a standing position then bow.
b. You join the bowing position immediately.
c. You wait for the imam to stand up.
d. You complete the prayer with the imam and make up that cycle.

If you arrive at a new location and plan to stay for more than four days:

a. Pray all prayers as shortened.
b. Continue to shorten your prayers.
c. Return to praying the regular number of cycles.
d. Combine all prayers in one time.

Who is required to attend the Friday prayer (Jumuah)?

a. Women, children, and travelers.
b. Only resident Muslim men.
c. The sick and the handicapped.
d. Any Muslim regardless of their status.

What should you do if you miss the Friday prayer?

a. Pray the sunset prayer (Maghrib).
b. Pray the midday prayer (Dhuhr) instead.
c. Combine the midday (dhuhr) and afternoon (asr) prayers.
d. Pray twice the next Friday.

Write the correct word.

1 The prayer of the traveler allows for _____ cycle prayers to be shortened.

2 The minimum amount of wealth required to pay zakah is the equivalent of _____ ounces of gold.

3 If you arrive at a new facility after traveling and plan to stay for more than _____ days, you must pray the regular number of cycles.

4 Shortening prayers for travel is allowed when traveling at least _____ miles.

5 _____ prayer cannot be combined with any other.

Other Prayer Topics + Zakah

What are some challenges your community faces with the Friday (Jumuah) prayer? How can you work together to overcome them? Reflect on the importance of this prayer.

Even though you might not be required to pay zakah, how can you actively participate in helping others within your capacity?

What are the most important things you learned/reviewed in this chapter?

This is an optional section.
Completing it is not necessary for the successful completion of this book.

Masjids Around the World – Art Therapy

Copy/draw, decorate or color this masjid while learning about it.

Hagia Sophia, Türkiye

The Hagia Sophia Masjid in Istanbul, Turkey, was originally built as a Christian cathedral in 537 AD. It was turned into a masjid after Ottoman rule in 1453, then a museum in 1935, and then was converted back to a masjid in 2020. It's known for its architecture, beautiful art, and history.

Fasting in Ramadan

MAIN POINTS

- The main purpose of fasting is to gain "taqwa" (God-consciousness).
- Ramadan is the month in which the Holy Quran was first revealed.
- Fasting in Islam is to abstain from food, drink, smoking, intoxication, and sexual intercourse or intentional ejaculation, from the morning prayer (Fajr) until the sunset prayer (Maghrib).

LEARNING OBJECTIVES

- To understand the importance and benefits of fasting
- To know how to fast, who should fast, and who should not
- To recognize what Zakat al-Fitr is and how it is applicable in, and outside of prison
- To know how to pray the Eid prayer alone and in a group

Reflection Questions

- Have you ever fasted in Ramadan? If so, how did fasting make you feel spiritually?
- If your first Ramadan is coming up, what are your biggest concerns?

Key Terms

- **Taqwa:** God-consciousnes. To be aware of Allah in every moment
- **Laylat al Qadr:** The Night of Power – we don't know the exact date of this night. We worship frequently in Ramadan in the hopes that we gain the reward of this night.
- **Suhoor:** The pre-dawn meal
- **Zakat al-fitr:** an obligatory alm at the end of Ramadan
- **Eid al-Fitr:** The celebration on the first day of the month following Ramadan
- **Khutba:** Islamic sermon
- **Eid Mubarak:** Blessed Eid

Fasting Ramadan

⟨O Believers! Fasting has been prescribed for you, just as it was prescribed
for those before you, that you may gain God-consciousness (taqwa).⟩
Quran 2:183

The fourth pillar of Islam is fasting during the
month of Ramadan. Ramadan is the ninth
month of the Islamic lunar year, and it is the
month in which the Quran was first revealed.

*Islamic months follow the lunar (moon) calendar,
which is shorter than the regular (solar) year. This is
why lunar months move about 10 days earlier each
year. The new moon signifies the beginning of a new
Islamic month.*

*There are two methods to make sure a new lunar
month is beginning: following eye-sightings or
following astronomical calculations. Those in prison
may follow calculations because seeing the moon
isn't always possible.*

⟨Ramadan is the month in which the Quran was revealed. Guidance for
humanity and clear proofs of guidance and criterion. So whoever of you
witnesses the month, let him fast it.⟩
Quran 2:185

Virtues of Ramadan

- It is the month in which the final revelation of Allah (the Quran) was revealed to humanity.
- The gates of paradise are opened, the gates of Hellfire are closed, and the devils are chained.
- Good deeds are given greater weight.
- All sins are forgiven. The Prophet ﷺ said, "Whosoever fasts in Ramadan with faith and seeking Allah's reward, all his past sins are forgiven."
- The Night of Power *(Laylat al Qadr)* is observed during this month. It is the exact night when the Holy Quran was revealed. Worshipping Allah during this night is better than 1,000 months of worship.

⟨The Night of Power is better than a thousand months.⟩
Quran 97:3

How to Fast

Fasting in Islam is to abstain from food, drink, sexual intercourse, intoxication, smoking, and intentional ejaculation from the beginning of dawn (Fajr) until the sun has completely set below the horizon (Maghrib).

It is highly recommended to eat or drink something– even small–before the time of Fajr prayer. The Prophet ﷺ said: "**Suhoor** [the pre-dawn meal] is a blessed meal, so do not omit it, even if one of you only takes a sip of water, for Allah and His Angels send blessings on those who eat suhoor."

It's important to not delay breaking one's fast once the sun has set.

The Prophet ﷺ said:
"The people will continue to do well so long as they hasten to break the fast."

It is very important to avoid bad speech and behaviors while fasting. The fast is valid but may be deficient in blessing. The Prophet ﷺ said: "Whoever does not give up false speech and acting upon it, and offensive speech and behavior, Allah has no need of his giving up his food and drink."

Pre-dawn meal

Fajr: Fast Begins

No food, drink, sexual intercourse or intentional ejaculation, intoxication or smoking

Maghrib: Fast ends

Post-fast meal

Isha (night prayer)

"Fasting is a shield; so when one of you is fasting he should neither indulge in obscene language nor should he raise his voice in anger. If someone attacks him or insults him, let him say: 'I am fasting!'"

You will learn more about good and bad speech in the Tayba course *Purify Your Speech*.

▥ Prison Context

Register as Muslim: Inform the chaplain in writing that you practice Islam.

Join the Religious Diet: Sign up for the Muslim diet offered by the prison.

Prepare for Ramadan: Start practicing fasting by reducing meals or fasting half a day.

Plan Ahead: Store some food for emergencies, focus on basic worship, and talk to the doctor if you have health issues. Make a manageable plan for worship in Ramadan.

Benefits of Fasting

People are made up of two parts: a physical body and a spiritual soul. Most of the time, we pay attention to the body's needs and wants, but forget about the soul. Fasting shifts the focus from physical things, like food, drink and desires, to our spiritual side, helping our faith in Allah and love for His Prophet ﷺ grow.

Fasting is spiritual training. Muslims control their desires to please Allah and try to do what the Quran says: "gain God-consciousness." Quran 2:183

Fasting helps us avoid doing wrong in two ways:

1. It reduces the energy that pushes us toward bad actions.
2. By actively giving up wrong actions while fasting.

Fasting also teaches us what hunger feels like, helping us to be more kind and caring toward people in poverty.

> **God-consciousness means to be aware of Allah in every moment of every day and to make decisions based on that awareness. How does controlling your desires for over 12 hours straight help you be constantly aware of Allah?**

_____

_____

_____

Who Must Fast?

Muslims that reached puberty must fast in the month of Ramadan. However, some people should not fast. Others are not allowed to fast.

🚫 These people do not fast:

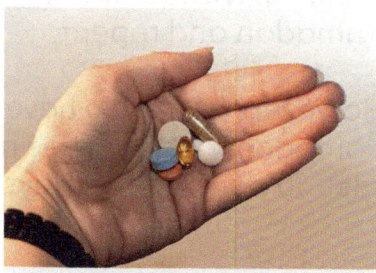

1. Those who are sick or injured such that fasting would be difficult or make their sickness worse. An example would be having a virus such as the flu.
2. Those who cannot fast due to old age, or chronic health reasons.
3. Travelers, if they choose to
4. Menstruating women and women experiencing postnatal bleeding are not allowed to fast. They make up the missed days after Ramadan. (Pregnant or nursing mothers should consult their doctors.)

A person who can become more unwell by changing the times of their medicine should not fast. But if one is able to change the times without harm, then this person should.

If a person gets better, or finishes their travel, then they make up the missed days after Ramadan fast.

What are some ways you can still benefit from Ramadan if you are unable to fast? Brainstorm some ideas even if you _can_ fast.

1

2

3

4

5

Things that Break the Fast

1. Eating or drinking on purpose. If you forget and eat or drink by accident, your fast is still valid.
2. Sexual intercourse or intentionally causing ejaculation (masturbation).
3. Ingesting anything on purpose, even if it's not food, like smoke or steam. However, if smoke is in the air from work or someone smoking, it doesn't break your fast. But try to avoid being near people while they smoke if you can.
4. Beginning the menstrual cycle or having postnatal bleeding.

What if a Person Purposely Breaks Their Fast?

Fasting during Ramadan is a command from Allah and is something we must do (unless one of the exceptions applies). If one purposely does not fast or breaks their fast by eating or drinking, without a valid reason, this is a grave issue. A person needs to make up the day after Ramadan and repent.

However – if people have intentional sexual intercourse during the daytime (fajr-maghrib) of Ramadan, both parties must make up the day. The person who performs penetration must fast 60 consecutive days as expiation to make up for this act.

Sexual intercourse outside of marriage is a grave sin in Islam. If one has done it, one should immediately seek forgiveness from Allah and repent for what they have done. Then the person should do their best to keep away from things that may lead them into falling into these actions again.

Zakah of Ending the Fast

In the last days of Ramadan, there is an obligatory alm called "The Obligatory Alm of Ramadan's End" *(Zakat al-Fitr)*. It must be given by anyone who has enough food to feed themselves for a day. Zakat al-Fitr can be paid in food (like 7lb of wheat, dates, barley, etc.) or the cash equivalent. One must also pay it for any family members one supports, like a wife, or children one has custody of.

As of Ramadan/March 2024 in America, the amount for Zakat al-Fitr is $10 per person.

▥ Zakat al-Fitr in the Prison Context

Zakat al-Fitr is meant to be given as the main food of your area. Since you're in prison, you can give things like ramen noodles, rice, or tuna pouches.

Make sure you are paying by the weight of the food, not the weight of the packaging.

While giving cash is allowed, most prisoners can't exchange cash. So, it's better to buy food from the commissary to give. If there is someone in charge of distributing Zakat al-Fitr, and they do it fairly, you can give them the food to pass on for you.

If you can't afford Zakat al-Fitr, you don't have to pay it.

Celebration After Ramadan: Eid al-Fitr

The celebration *(Eid al-Fitr)* is on the first day after Ramadan ends—the first of Shawwal (10th lunar month). It begins with worship as the entire community comes together, prays the Eid prayer, listens to a sermon *(khutba)*, and gives thanks to Allah for the immense blessings gained from Ramadan. After the sermon, Muslims wish each other *(Eid Mubarak)* "blessed Eid" and enjoy the rest of the day, often with friends and loved ones, while in the remembrance of Allah. It's important to note that while Eid is a day of celebration, this does not mean it's a day to be heedless and forget about Allah, it's quite the opposite.

▥ Eid al-Fitr in the Prison Context

In prison, sometimes Muslims are not able to pray the Eid prayer together. If this happens, they should pray together in the housing unit in the largest group possible, even if it is only two people. If there is only one Muslim in the unit, this person should pray the 2 cycles of Eid prayer by themselves.

The Eid prayer is performed the same way as a regular two-cycle prayer, except that it includes additional mentions of "Allahu Akbar" in the standing position. This prayer must be performed before noon on that specific day.

When praying alone:

First Cycle
→ Stand for prayer + say Allahu Akbar to begin
→ Say "Allahu Akbar" six more times
→ Recite Al-Fatiha and continue this cycle as usual

Second Cycle
→ Stand after completing the first cycle
→ Say "Allahu Akbar" five times
→ Recite Recite Al-Fatiha and continue this cycle as usual

When praying in a group:

If you are able to pray in a group, the Imam will usually describe how the Eid prayer is to be performed before the prayer begins. In that case, just follow what he says, even if it is different from what we described here. There are various schools of thought and thus slightly different ways to perform the prayer.

If the prison administration allows it, the Muslims should celebrate by having a meal with each other sometime during the day or night, even if it is on a different day than Eid. However, the Eid prayer must be performed on the exact day of Eid. Muslims should eat or drink something small before the Eid prayer, such as a date or water.

Fasts Outside of Ramadan

The Prophet ﷺ also fasted at other times aside from the month of Ramadan such as on Mondays and Thursdays along with other days that he specified. This will be be discussed in the more advanced courses.

Pilgrimage (Hajj)

The fifth pillar of Islam is pilgrimage (Hajj). It necessitates traveling to Makkah. You will study more about this in further Tayba courses. When Allah wills it, you will make the journey.

Fasting in Ramadan

Write two benefits of fasting.

1

2

Write (T) for True and (F) for False.

1   Ramadan is the month in which the Quran was first revealed.

2   Good deeds are given greater weight in Ramadan.

3   Fasting starts at Dhuhr prayer and ends at Isha prayer.

4   Muslims are encouraged to fast only in Ramadan.

5   If a person forgetfully eats or drinks something while fasting, their fast is still valid and they should continue the fast.

6   Eid al-Fitr begins on the last day of Ramadan.

Write 2 situations where fasting during Ramadan is not required.

1

2

What should a Muslim do if they intentionally break their fast to smoke?

Fasting in Ramadan

How does fasting during Ramadan help you understand and care more about people who have less?

What are some steps you can take to make sure you benefit as much as you can from Ramadan in prison?

What are some of the most important things you learned/reviewed in this chapter?

This is an optional section.
Completing it is not necessary for the successful completion of this book.

Masjids Around the World – Art Therapy

Copy/draw, decorate or color this masjid while learning about it.

Niujie Masjid, Beijing

The Niujie Masjid, the oldest and largest masjid in Beijing, was originally built in 996 during the Liao dynasty and has been rebuilt and expanded several times since. Located in the Niujie area of Beijing, it combines traditional Chinese and Islamic architectural styles and can hold over 1,000 worshippers. The masjid reflects a rich history and serves as a core Islamic center for Beijing's Muslim community.

The Six Pillars of Belief

MAIN POINTS

The 6 Pillars of Belief (or 6 articles of faith) are believing in Allah, His Angels, His revealed Books, His Messengers, the Last Day, and predestination.

LEARNING OBJECTIVES

- To identify the 6 Pillars of Belief in Islam
- To identify unique attributes of Allah
- To describe characteristics of angels
- To name specific angels and their duties
- To summarize the events of the Last Day
- To recognize both destiny and free will

Reflection Questions

- When you reflect on Allah, what attributes of Allah first come to your mind?
- Which of the the 6 pillars of belief did you believe in before you accepted Islam?
- Which beliefs did you accept after becoming a Muslim?

Key Terms

- **Qadr:** predestination - everything that happens is destined by Allah

The 6 Pillars of Belief (Iman)

In Chapter 1 we learned about the Hadith of Jibril. It mentions the 6 pillars of belief:

1. Belief in Allah
2. Belief in His Angels
3. Belief in His revealed Scriptures/Books
4. Belief in His Messengers
5. Belief in the Last Day
6. Belief in Predestination (fate), whether good or bad

This chapter introduces each of them. They will be covered in more depth in the next course, *Iman 99*.

IMAN

Belief in Allah

Belief in The Angels

Belief in the Books

Belief in the Messengers

Belief in the Last Day

Belief in Fate/Divine Decree

What is something that you've seen or learned about that made you marvel at the power and creation of Allah?

1 - Belief in Allah

The most important belief for a Muslim is the Oneness of Allah. Every Muslim has been commanded by Allah in the Quran:

❴**Know that there is no God but Allah.**❵
Quran 47:19

This means to know without any doubt that He is One, without any partners or children.

<u>Who is Allah?</u>

Allah is the Arabic word for God, the Creator of the heavens, the earth, and everything that exists. Some people think Muslims believe in a different God because we say "Allah." But "Allah" is simply the name God uses for Himself in the Quran. The word "Allah" is special because it can't be made plural and has no gender. When we say Allah, we mean the same God worshiped by Abraham, Moses, Jesus, and Muhammad ﷺ.

Allah is One and can't be divided. He has no equal, no partner, and no one can share in His power. Allah doesn't have children, parents, or anyone like Him. He is completely unique, and nothing can compare to Him.

We can't fully understand the true nature of Allah. He has no beginning or end and isn't limited by time. He is the only God, and He is the Most Merciful.

The name of Allah in Arabic calligraphy

❴ **Say, [O Prophet] "He is Allah—One [and Indivisible]; Allah—the Sustainer [needed by all]. He has never had offspring, nor was He born. And there is none comparable to Him.** ❵
Quran 112:1-4

<u>Common Misconceptions</u>

Because of different cultures and beliefs, some Muslims—whether new or not—use phrases that disrespect the greatness of Allah. It's very important to remove these from your heart, mind, and speech:

×   "The old man"
×   "The man upstairs"
×   Referring to Allah as a female. Likewise with considering Allah as a male (even though Allah refers to Himself as "He" in the Quran), but Allah is neither male nor female.
×   Referring to a sport star as a god, even if it is said metaphorically.
×   Referring to Jesus (Prophet 'Isa) as God, or the son of God.
×   Mentioning Allah when cursing, like saying "G*ddamn!"

All of these and similar expressions should be totally abandoned.

2 - Belief In the Angels

Angels are a mighty creation of Allah made from light, and they are completely obedient to Him. They do not have free will to choose disobedience of Allah.

❴ ...the Angels, and they are not arrogant. They fear their Lord above them, and do what they are commanded. ❵
Quran 16:49-50

→ They do not eat or drink
→ They are not male or female
→ They do not have children
→ The do not feel desires like human beings

The Quran mentions that they have wings: some with two; others three or four.

❴ ...Who made angels ˹as His˺ messengers with wings—two, three, or four...❵
Quran 35:1

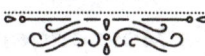

<u>The Well-Known Angels</u>

There are ten angels mentioned by name in the Quran and Sunnah.

Name		Assigned Role
1	Jibril (Gabriel)	Brings divine revelation to the Prophets of Allah
2	Mikaeel (Michael)	In charge of the rain and clouds
3	Izraeel (Azrael)	In charge of taking the souls of those who die
4	Israfil (Raphael)	Will blow the trumpet to start the Day of Judgment
5 & 6	Raqeeb and Ateed	The titles of two angels that are with you at all times recording all that you say and do. One is on your right side recording your good deeds, while the other is on your left side recording your bad deeds.
7 & 8	Munkar and Nakeer	Two angels who will visit you in your grave and question you about three matters: Who is your Lord? What is your way of life? And Who is your Prophet?
9	Ridwan	In charge of the gates of Paradise
10	Malik	In charge of the gates of Hell

<u>Clearing Up Common Misconceptions</u>

The Quran makes it clear that Satan is not an angel. Rather he is from another type of creation called "jinn".

Angels never disobey because they do not have free will. But jinn, who are created from smokeless fire, have free will—like human beings. They have the choice to obey or disobey the commandments of Allah.

❴ We said to the angels, 'Bow down before Adam,' and they all bowed down, but not Iblis [Satan]: he was one of the jinn and he disobeyed his Lord's command ❵
Quran 18:50

3 - Belief in His Revealed Scriptures/Books

As Muslims, we believe the Quran is the word of Allah, revealed to the Prophet Muhammad ﷺ through the Angel Jibril. We also believe that Allah revealed other scriptures before the Quran.

❴O believers! Have faith in Allah, His Messenger, the Book He has revealed to His Messenger, and the Scriptures He revealed before. Indeed, whoever denies Allah, His angels, His Books, His messengers, and the Last Day has clearly gone far astray.❵
Quran 4:136

Allah has always sent guidance to people through revelation. But over time, people would forget or change the scriptures.

❴There are some among them who distort the Book with their tongues to make you think this ˹distortion˺ is from the Book—but it is not what the Book says. They say, "It is from Allah"—but it is not from Allah. And ˹so˺ they attribute lies to Allah knowingly.❵
Quran 3:78

Out of His mercy, Allah continued to send prophets and messengers with scripture to explain how we should live. This ended with the Quran, the final revelation to Prophet Muhammad ﷺ.

Allah also promised to protect the Quran from any changes until the Day of Judgment.

❴Indeed, it is We Who sent down the Dhikr (i.e. the Quran) and surely, We will guard it (from corruption)❵
Quran 15:9

إِنَّا نَحْنُ نَزَّلْنَا الذِّكْرَ وَإِنَّا لَهُ لَحَافِظُونَ ۝

Calligraphy of verse 15:9

<u>Clearing up Common Misconceptions</u>

Even though Muslims believe in earlier scriptures that came before the Quran, the earlier scriptures have been corrupted. They are currently not in their original forms.

Thus, we must make sure they do not contradict anything in the Quran or Hadith. It's important to know that the Quran is the last Revelation sent to humankind. There will never be another divine book after it. It is our guide of all the Divine Books and contains the essence of them all.

4 - Belief in the Messengers

The most noble of human beings are the Prophets and Messengers. The Prophets and Messengers are those obedient servants chosen by Allah to receive revelation.

All Prophets and Messengers received revelation from Allah. The Messengers were also commanded to spread the message of faith to their communities. Every messenger is a prophet, but not every prophet is a messenger.

❴**We surely sent a messenger to every community, saying, "Worship Allah and shun false gods." But some of them were guided by Allah, while others were destined to stray. So travel throughout the land and see the fate of the deniers!**❵
Quran 16:36

When the Messenger of Allah, Muhammad ﷺ, was asked about how many prophets had been sent to humankind, he replied, "124,000." When he ﷺ was asked how many messengers were sent, he replied, "313."

So, there were a large number of prophets and messengers sent to all of humankind throughout the ages, all over the world and their mission was to convey to the people the truth of the Oneness of Allah, His laws, and the next life.

<u>Prophets and Messengers in the Quran</u>

There are 25 prophets and messengers mentioned in the Quran.

Adam	Idris	Nuh	Ibrahim	Hud
	(Enoch)	(Noah)	(Abraham)	(Eber)
Quran 2:31	Quran 19:56	Quran 6:89	Quran 19:41	Quran 26:125
Salih	Lut	Ismail	Ishaq	Yaqub
(Shelah)	(Lot)	(Ishmael)	(Isaac)	(Jacob)
Quran 26:143	Quran 6:86	Quran 19:54	Quran 19:49	Quran 19:49
Ayyub	Dhul-Kifl	Shuayb	Yusuf	Musa
(Job)	(Ezekial)	(Jethro)	(Joseph)	(Moses)
Quran 4:89	Quran 21:85-86	Quran 26:178	Quran 12:7	Quran 19:51
Harun	Yunus	Dawud	Sulayman	Zakariyya
(Aaron)	(Jonah)	(David)	(Solomon)	(Zakaria)
Quran 19:53	Quran 6:89	Quran 6:89	Quran 6:89	Quran 6:89
Ilyaas	Al-Yasa	Yahya	Isa	Muhammad
(Elijah)	(Elisha)	(John)	(Jesus)	(ﷺ)
Quran 6:89	Quran 6:89	Quran 3:39	Quran 19:30	

The Necessary Characteristics of Prophets and Messengers

Prophets and messengers are protected from making major or minor sins. They have five key qualities:

1. Truthfulness
2. Trustworthiness
3. Intelligence
4. Sinlessness
5. Proper conveyance of the divine message

These traits make them perfect role models for humankind. It's impossible for them to have opposite traits because they were chosen to receive revelation from Allah.

Clearing up Common Misconceptions

Two points need to be clarified:

1. In popular religious movements, leaders are often described as "prophets". Just because someone had true dreams or predicted the future, it does not mean he is a prophet of Allah. No one can become a prophet of Allah by their own will. Also, the final prophet and messenger is Prophet Muhammad ﷺ and there will be no more after him.

Calligraphy of the name of the Final Prophet and Messenger: Muhammad ﷺ

2. As mentioned before, the prophets and messengers were the first to follow divine guidance and had excellent morals. However, in the Bible, there are some stories about prophets that show them behaving in ways that don't match their high moral standards. As Muslims, we believe these stories are changes or corruptions made to the original scriptures. Some examples include:

✗ They accuse a specific Prophet of appearing drunk and indecent around his son.
✗ They accuse a specific Prophet of committing unspeakable acts with his daughters.
✗ They accuse a specific Prophet of behaving immorally and causing the death of his general.

These are just a few examples. As Muslims, we reject any descriptions of the prophets that are disrespectful or go against the divine guidance they followed. We ask Allah to protect us from disrespecting anything that we should hold in high esteem.

5 - Belief in the Last Day

The Quran is filled with verses that remind us that life, as we know it, will come to an end.

This last day has many names in the Quran such as:

→ the Day of Standing (Yawm al-Qiyama),

→ The Striking Disaster (Al-Qari'a),

→ The Gathering (Al-Hashr), and

→ The Overwhelming Event (Al-Waqi'a).

❴The Striking Disaster! What is the Striking Disaster? And what will make you realize what the Striking Disaster is? ˹It is˺ the Day people will be like scattered moths, and the mountains will be like carded wool.❵

Quran 101:1-5

❴When the sun is put out, and when the stars fall down, and when the mountains are blown away, and when pregnant camels are left untended, and when wild beasts are gathered together, and when the seas are set on fire, and when the souls ˹and their bodies˺ are paired ˹once more˺, and when baby girls, buried alive, are asked for what crime they were put to death, and when the records ˹of deeds˺ are laid open, and when the sky is stripped away, and when the Hellfire is fiercely flared up, and when Paradise is brought near— ˹on that Day˺ each soul will know what ˹deeds˺ it has brought along.❵

Quran 81:1-14

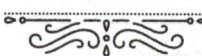

In these verses and others like them, Allah describes the end of the universe. As these events happen, people will be terrified by what they see, with even infants turning gray-haired from fear.

Then, Allah will command the Angel Israfil to blow the trumpet. This sound will be so terrifying that all living things will die. After some time, Israfil will blow the trumpet again, and this will bring back to life every person who ever existed.

The Day of Judgment

After resurrection, all people will be placed in ranks according to their deeds. Everyone will be handed a book of deeds that will contain every action ever done in their lives—big or small, good or bad. If it contains mostly good, the person will rejoice. If it contains mostly bad, the person will feel deep regret.

People's deeds will be weighed on a divine scale. They will give an account of everything in their life, especially 5 things:

→ their life and how they spent it,
→ their youth and how they used it,
→ their wealth and how they earned it and spent it,
→ and how they practiced what they knew.

Reflect on these 5 now in your life. What can you do to improve on each one?

Your life and how you spent it so far:

Your youth and how you use(d) it:

Your wealth and how you earn it and spend it:

How you practice what you know:

After the Scales

After our actions are weighed, we will have to pass over a bridge that is set over the Hellfire. Some will pass over quickly, others just barely, and some will fall into the Fire. Lastly, everyone will be either rewarded for their faith and good deeds with Paradise or punished for their disbelief and sins with Hellfire.

6 - Belief in Predestination *(Qadr)*

The final pillar of belief deals with predestination (qadr), or destiny/fate.

Whatever happens in the universe or to a person was destined by Allah. It could not have been any other way. Allah is the One who has determined every outcome, whether good or bad.

⟨**When We intend for something to happen, We say to it, 'Be,' and it becomes.**⟩
Quran 16:40

These verses indicate that nothing comes into existence, has ability, lives, or dies without the will of Allah.

What About Free Will?

On the flip side is that people have free will. We are rewarded and punished based on how we use our free will.

⟨**Allah burdens not a person beyond his scope. He gets reward for that (good) which he has earned, and he is punished for that (evil) which he has earned.**⟩
Quran 2:286

Decisions and reactions take us in different directions in life.

If a person decides to disobey Allah, he is given the ability to do so through the power and permission of Allah, even though he has displeased his Lord. There is no power or ability except through Allah. Our deeds will be for us or against us, depending on our intentions.

Humans are responsible for their actions and will be judged as to how they used their free will.

The Six Pillars of Belief

What are the 6 Pillars of Belief in Islam?

Write (T) for True and (F) for False.

1   The most important belief of Islam is the Oneness of Allah.

2   Angels are made of white clay.

3   Angels always obey Allah.

4   Satan is a fallen angel.

5   There will be no more prophets or messengers after the Prophet Muhammad ﷺ.

6   Today's Bible contains untrue stories of prophets.

Name 3 angels and their assigned role:

1

2

3

Name 2 necessary characteristics of prophets and messengers.

1

2

The Six Pillars of Belief

Pick one of the five necessary characteristics of Prophets and Messengers. What is the opposite of this characteristic? Why would this not be possible for a Prophet?

Why do you think it's important to recognize that people have free will?

What are some of the most important things you learned/reviewed in this chapter?

This is an optional section.
Completing it is not necessary for the successful completion of this book.

Masjids Around the World – Art Therapy

Copy/draw, decorate or color this masjid while learning about it.

Great Mosque of Djenné, Mali

The Great Mosque of Djenné is a famous example of Sudano-Sahelian architecture. It is made mostly of adobe. The first masjid was built in the 13th century, but the current building was completed in 1907. It was designated a UNESCO World Heritage Site in 1988. The local community plays a big role in taking care of the masjid.

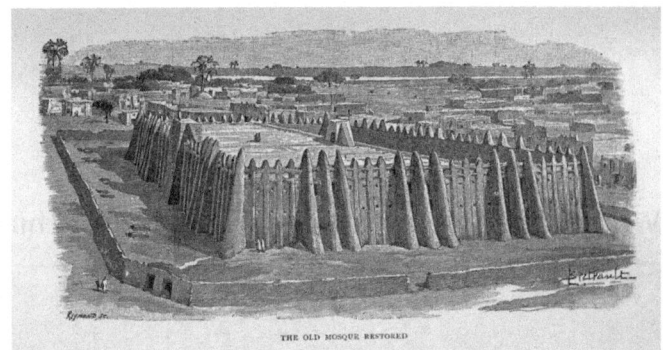

THE OLD MOSQUE RESTORED

Excellence (Ihsan)

MAIN POINTS

- Ihsan (excellence) is an essential part of our religion (dīn).
- The people of Ihsan are described in the Quran.
- Ihsan means trying to please Allah in everything we do—what we think, feel, do, or avoid doing. It is that you worship Allah as if you see Him. If you don't see Him, know that He sees you.

LEARNING OBJECTIVES

- To define Ihsan and understand its two levels.
- To explore how Ihsan applies to one's practice of Islam.
- To distinguish between obligatory and non-obligatory Ihsan.
- To understand Ihsan as it applies to worship and interactions.

Reflection Questions

- What is an example of excellence that you have seen or experienced?
- Why is doing outward actions not enough to be true Muslims?

Key Terms

- **Ihsan:** excellence – aiming to please Allah in everything we do

What is Ihsan?

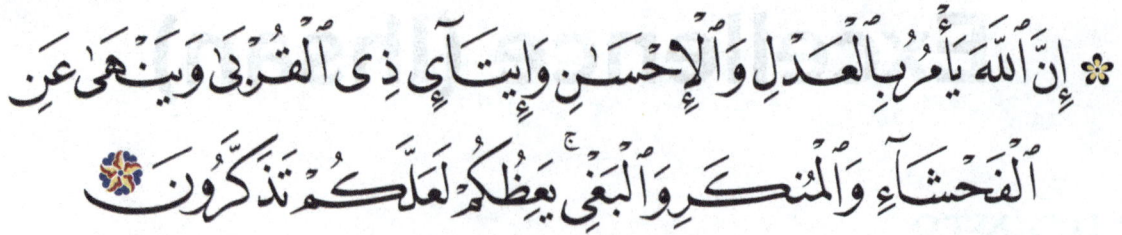

﴿Indeed, Allah commands justice and excellence (Ihsan), as well as generosity to close relatives. He forbids indecency, wickedness, and aggression. He instructs you so perhaps you will be mindful.﴾
Quran 16:90

Ihsan means trying to please Allah in everything we do—what we think, feel, do, or avoid doing.

Ihsan is about always being aware of Allah and only doing things that would please Allah.

Ihsan also means striving for excellence in our faith (Iman) and our worship (Islam). It applies to all parts of our lives, including how we treat others and how we approach everything we do.

Having Ihsan means doing what is required of us in the best way we can and always trying to improve. Ihsan is about going above and beyond: doing more than just what's required. For example, it's not only treating others fairly but being extra kind to them.

As mentioned in Hadith Jibril, Ihsan is one of the three essential elements of the religion (dīn). It's important to know that all three elements need to be present in a Muslim.

The People of Ihsan

Excellence (Ihsan) is mentioned 191 times in the Quran. Allah is telling us not only to believe and worship, but to excel (have Ihsan) in all that we do.

The following are some examples where Allah mentions the people of excellence (Ihsan). As you read through this selection of verses, notice the descriptions Allah is giving us about Ihsan and the people of Ihsan. Picture what type of person Allah is describing and encouraging us to be:

﴿Indeed Whoever submits themselves to Allah and is a person of Ihsan will have their reward with their Lord. And there will be no fear for them, nor will they grieve.﴾
Quran 2:112

﴿Spend in the cause of Allah. Do not let your own hands throw you into destruction. And do good (Ihsan), for Allah certainly loves the good-doers (people of Ihsan).﴾
Quran 2:195

⟪And who is better in faith than those who ˹fully˺ submit themselves to Allah, do good (Ihsan), and follow the Way of Abraham, the upright? Allah chose Abraham as a close friend⟫

4:125

⟪When they listen to what has been revealed to the Messenger, you see their eyes overflowing with tears for recognizing the truth. They say, "Our Lord! We believe, so count us among the witnesses. Why should we not believe in Allah and the truth that has come to us? And we long for our Lord to include us in the company of the righteous." So Allah will reward them for what they said with Gardens under which rivers flow, to stay there forever. And that is the reward of the good-doers (people of Ihsan).⟫

Quran 5:83-85

⟪... Surely whoever is mindful ˹of Allah˺ and patient, then certainly Allah never discounts the reward of those who do Ihsan.⟫

Quran 12:90

⟪Indeed Allah is with those who have taqwa and those who are people of Ihsan.⟫

Quran 16:128

⟪Indeed, the righteous will be amid Gardens and springs, ˹joyfully˺ receiving what their Lord will grant them. Before this ˹reward˺ they were truly good-doers (people of Ihsan) ˹in the world˺: they used to sleep only little in the night, and pray for forgiveness before dawn. And in their wealth there was a rightful share ˹fulfilled˺ for the one who asks and the one who needs but doesn't ask.⟫

Quran 51:15-19

What do those people Allah is describing seem like to you?

What areas are you strong in your Ihsan?

What areas of your Ihsan could use improvement?

Two Levels of Ihsan

The Messenger of Allah ﷺ perfected Ihsan. When he ﷺ was asked to define Ihsan, he ﷺ said, "That you worship Allah as if you see Him. If you don't see Him, know that He sees you."

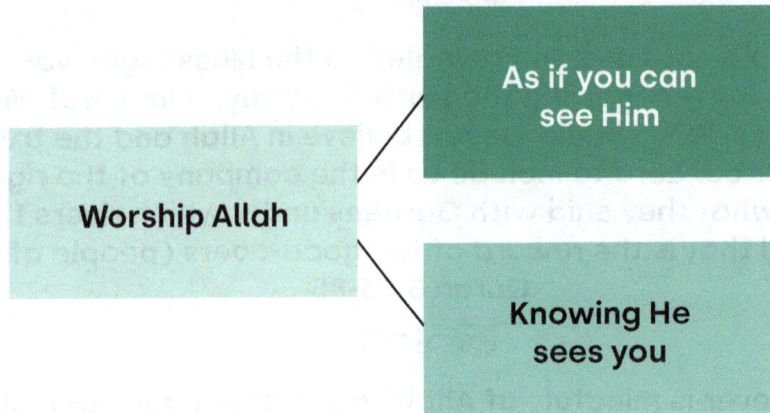

These two levels are higher than just doing an act of worship. If we worship without these levels, we might fulfill the basic requirements of Islam. But when we worship with either of these levels, we are showing Ihsan (excellence) in that act.

Take a moment to describe prayer and what it might look like at the two levels, and if neither of those levels are present.

Prayer	
Worshiping as if you can see Allah	
Worshiping knowing that He sees you	
Worshiping with neither of those two levels	

Understanding Ihsan through Everyday Examples

We know that Allah bears no resemblance whatsoever to His creation. At the same time, we can use examples from our life to better understand concepts in our religion.

To understand this idea of the two levels of Ihsan, think about how you act when someone like a teacher, prison guard, or warden is watching you. When you can see them watching, you're more careful, right? Even if you can't see them but know they're watching, you're still focused. But how would you act if you didn't feel their presence at all?

This helps explain the idea of Ihsan. To worship Allah is if we can see Him and to always be aware that Allah is watching, even if you can't see Him.

Teacher Example	How would you be if you were taking a test?
You can see the teacher right in front of you.	
You can't see the teacher, but you know for sure the teacher can see you.	
You can't see the teacher and you are not aware that the teacher can see you.	

Officer Example	How would you act on a job if your officer entrusts you with a certain material to use?
You can see the officer right in front of you.	
You can't see the officer, but you know for sure the officer can see you.	
You can't see the officer and you are not aware that the officer can see you.	

Ihsan in Worship and Interactions

In our lives, we worship Allah and have interactions with other people. In both areas of worship and interactions, we strive to have Ihsan.

Examples of worship are:	Examples of interactions are:
• Prayer • Fasting • Charity • Pilgrimage • Reciting Quran	• Business transactions • Marriage • Speaking with other people • Working with other people • Sharing common spaces

Take a moment to describe what business transactions might look like at the two levels and also if neither of those levels are present.

Business Transactions (buying/selling/trade)	
As if you can see Allah	
Knowing that He sees you	
With neither of those two levels	

Two Types of Ihsan

We should have Ihsan in all our actions whether they are required and recommended.

Types of Actions and Their Rulings		
	Worship	**Interaction**
Obligatory (required)	• Five daily prayers • Fasting Ramadan • Obligatory alms (zakat)	• Respecting parents • Taking care of one's spouse and children • Taking care of animals we own • Preserving our wealth • Fulfilling our business contracts and commitments
Recommended	• Extra prayers (sunna/nafila) • Fasting outside of Ramadan • Extra charity	• Showing extra kindness to our family • Being generous with guests and travellers • Giving gifts

Choose one required act and one recommended act. Describe them with the two levels of Ihsan and also without any Ihsan.

Required Action:	
As if you can see Allah	
Knowing that He sees you	
With neither of those two levels	

Recommended Action:	
As if you can see Allah	
Knowing that He sees you	
With neither of those two levels	

Ihsan to Your Neighbor

The Prophet Muhammad ﷺ said, "Whoever believes in Allah and the Last Day should be excellent (have Ihsan) with his neighbor." In another version of the Hadith, he said, "Whoever believes in Allah and the Last Day should not harm his neighbor."

Let's look at a famous story of one of the early Imams of the First Generations after the Prophet ﷺ and Companions. The Imam is Imam Abu Hanifa and he was one of the most righteous and knowledgeable people of the entire Muslim Ummah (nation) of his time and all time.

Imam Abu Hanifa would spend his days teaching and maintaining his business. He was also a judge among people. He would spend his nights praying and reciting Quran. His neighbor used to drink wine every night and sing very loudly, disturbing the Imam.

One night, Imam Abu Hanifa did not hear the man singing and so he asked around. The people said that he was arrested and taken to jail. Abu Hanifa, one of the most famous scholars and judges of his time, went down to the jail to ask about the man and to see how he was doing. When the ruler of that area found out that Imam Abu Hanifa visited the man in jail, he ordered that the man be released. The man later asked Abu Hanifa why he visited him in jail even though his drinking and singing bothered him every night. Abu Hanifa said, "Because you have a right upon me as a neighbor, and I have not been neglectful of that."

Maybe your neighbor is a cellmate, someone who is near you in a dorm, or someone in a cell close by.

How do you have Ihsan with your neighbor?

What would it look like for you to not harm your neighbor?

Excellence (Ihsan)

In your own words, describe Ihsan.

Write down some ideas on how you can increase in Ihsan in your life.

What are the 2 levels of Ihsan?

Write (T) for True and (F) for False.

1		Ihsan means trying to please Allah in everything we do—what we think, feel, do, or avoid doing.
2		Ihsan only applies to acts of worship.
3		You can, and should, have Ihsan in your interactions with others.
4		The Prophet Muhammad ﷺ said that whoever believes in Allah and the Last Day should have excellence (Ihsan) with their neighbor.
5		Worshiping Allah with Ihsan means you worship as if you can see Him, and if you don't see Him, knowing He sees you.

Excellence (Ihsan)

Reflect on the fact that Allah sees you at all times. How is this a higher level of Iman (faith) than just believing Allah exists?

What would be a situation where a neighbor is doing something harmful to you and you respond with Ihsan?

What are some of the most important things you learned/reviewed in this chapter?

Developing Ihsan: Tools of the Path

MAIN POINTS

- Internal and external tools are essential for developing Ihsan.
- Tawba (repentance) and Taqwa (God-consciousness) are the foundational tools.
- External tools include; protecting obligatory acts (fard), doing Dhikr (remembrance of Allah), seeking knowledge, and guarding the pathways of the heart.
- Internal tools include: love for the Prophet ﷺ, curing the diseases of the heart, and adorning the heart with stations of excellence.
- Long-lasting change requires: guidance from good company, sincerity, avoiding doubtful matters, and constant self-evaluation.

LEARNING OBJECTIVES

- To implement some of the main tools of developing Ihsan.
- To explain how repentance (Tawba) and Taqwa serve as a starting point for developing Ihsan.
- To understand what Taqwa is and its two levels.
- To implement external practices that lead to a deliberate state of developing Ihsan.
- To reflect on how internal tools contribute to deepening faith and achieving Ihsan.

Reflection Questions

- Reflect on the influence of the people around you. Are there any people that help you be a better person?
- What changes would you like to see in yourself?
- What are some traits you like and dislike in yourself?

Key Terms

- **Tawba:** Repentance
- **Taqwa:** Obeying the commands and avoiding the prohibitions of Allah, both outwardly and inwardly
- **Fard:** The required actions as a Muslim
- **Dhikr:** Remembrance of Allah

The Path of Ihsan

You already have Ihsan in your life. There are areas where you have excelled in your belief and worship of Allah. There are areas where you have excelled and have Ihsan in some ways that you interact with others. And there are other areas of your belief, worship and interactions with others that you need to work on.

We must go from a state where we have Ihsan here and there, to a state where we are deliberate of having and developing Ihsan.

When you actively put yourself into a conscious state that you want to excel in your faith (Iman) and actions (Islam), you are on the path of excellence (Ihsan).

| Occasional Ihsan in worship and interactions | Developing a conscious state of Ihsan in faith and actions |

List out some areas of strength and other areas where you need improvement as it relates to Ihsan. Think about worship and interactions.

Types of Actions and Their Rulings		
	Areas of Strength	**Areas that need improvement**
Worship	1. 2. 3.	1. 2. 3.
Interactions	1. 2. 3.	1. 2. 3.

Tools of the Path

As you travel this path of Ihsan, you will need tools and guides. In this chapter, we will cover some of the main tools that you will use as you develop your Ihsan.
Here is a list of some of the most important tools you will need:

1. Repentance *(Tawba)*
2. *(Taqwa)*
3. Protect the Outward Requirements *(fard)*
4. Remembering Allah *(Dhikr)*
5. Love of the Prophet Muhammad ﷺ
6. Seeking Knowledge
7. Guarding the Pathways to the Heart
8. Curing the Diseases of the Heart
9. Adorning the heart with the stations of excellence
10. The 6 M's
11. Avoiding the Doubtful
12. Guides and Fellows
13. Sincerity

Imagine trying to build a house without any tools—it wouldn't be possible.

Similarly, developing Ihsan requires specific tools. Without them, our Ihsan remains incomplete.

Which of the tools listed above do you most want to learn about?

What do you think is the reason you chose that tool?

Repentance (Tawba)

⟨Turn to Allah in repentance all together, O believers, so that you may be successful⟩
Quran 24:31

⟨O believers! Turn to Allah in sincere repentance, so your Lord may absolve
you of your sins and admit you into Gardens, under which rivers flow⟩
Quran 66:8

Repentance (tawba) is one of the main tools of the path. It is the first stage that a person must really look at as they embark on the path of Ihsan. We need to take a close look at the wrong things we are doing and the good things we are not doing. After that, we start the process of repentance for each mistake.

Through the process of regular and renewed repentance (tawba) you will be constantly purifying your soul as well as humbling it.

Every time we repent (make tawba) we are reminding ourselves that we are falling short of what we need to do. This not only humbles us, but it also drives us to continue *excelling*, which is Ihsan. We cannot improve something if we believe ourselves to be already excellent.

Think about the advancement of technology. No matter how good something is, there is always room for improvement. If an industry stops trying to excel in what they make, they will lose Ihsan in their product and they will be eventually rendered obsolete. In the same way, we constantly strive to excel in our worship of Allah. No matter how good we feel it is, there is ALWAYS room for improvement.

There are four conditions for repentance (tawba) to be sound:

1. Remorse
2. Intention to never do that action again
3. Stopping that action
4. Righting wrongs

1. <u>Remorse:</u> Only when we feel remorse for a sin can the process of tawba begin. If we stop an action because it's not good for our health, causes shame, or anything else, that is not true remorse. True remorse is only felt when we experience a strong feeling of sadness and regret and hate what we have done.

2. <u>Intention to never do that action again:</u> This is having a sincere and serious intention to never do that action again. Once you have that firm resolve to never do that thing again, you have fulfilled this condition of repentance (tawba).

3. <u>Stopping that action:</u> Sometimes, we do our repentance (tawba) after an action is done. If we are in the middle of committing a sin, we are commanded to stop that action and repent. If we do not stop that action and make tawba, now we have two sins: the sin of the action, and the sin of delaying the process of tawba.

4. <u>Righting wrongs:</u> Sometimes the sin we are repenting for is only between us and Allah. Examples would be like missing a prayer or eating something unlawful. Other times, our repentance is from a sin that involved another person. Examples would be like taking something that belongs to another person or slandering a person. If our sin involved another person, then this 4th condition applies: We have to right our wrongs. We have to give back the right we took or ask that the person to forgive us for what we did to them, said about them, or took from them.

When we repent (make tawba) that fulfills these four conditions, we firmly believe that Allah will accept that repentance and purify us from the sin. This is part of having a good opinion of Allah, that we remain hopeful in His Mercy towards us.

The Messenger of Allah ﷺ said, "The one who repents before the sun rises from its place of setting [from the West] shall have his repentance accepted by Allah." (Muslim)

While the above four conditions are all that are required for a tawba to be sound and valid, there are other things that one may do while seeking forgiveness. Examples are:

→ Saying, "Astaghfirullah" (I seek forgiveness from Allah)
→ Go back to the place of sin and do an act of worship there (unless doing so would be harmful).
→ Give out charity.
→ Pray an extra two cycles of prayer.

Taqwa

❴O believers! Have Taqwa of Allah in the way He deserves and do not die except that you are Muslims❵
Quran 3:102

❴Have Taqwa of Allah to the best of your ability, hear and obey, and spend in charity—that will be best for you. And whoever is saved from the selfishness of their own souls, it is they who are successful.❵
Quran 64:16

The Prophet ﷺ said, "(Actions that) admit people to Paradise the most are Taqwa and good character." (Tirmidhi)

The term Taqwa is mentioned in the Quran 258 times, both as a noun and a verb. You may see "Taqwa" translated in various ways. Some of them might include:

- God-consciousness
- Being mindful of Allah
- Fear of Allah
- Protection

We are choosing to not translate the term Taqwa since it is a term that is comprehensive of a number of meanings. A summary of the term Taqwa is as follows:

Taqwa is obeying the commands and avoiding the prohibitions of Allah, both outwardly and inwardly.

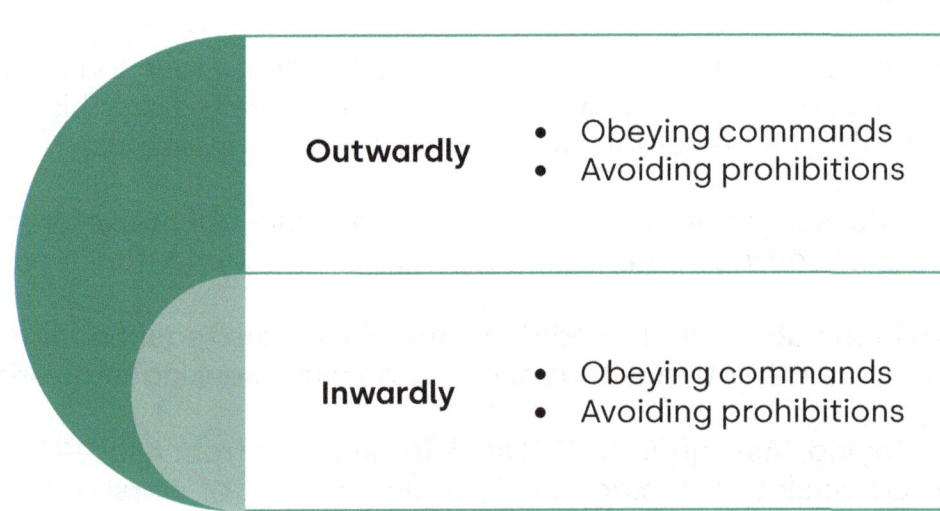

Outwardly	• Obeying commands • Avoiding prohibitions
Inwardly	• Obeying commands • Avoiding prohibitions

Examples of Taqwa

	Obey the commands	Avoid the prohibitions
Outwardly	• Prayer • Fasting • Obligatory alms • Honesty • Honoring Parents	• Backbiting • Carrying tales • False testimony • Lying • Cheating
Inwardly	• Sincerity • Repentance (Tawbah) • Patience • Gratitude • Depending on Allah	• Religious showing off • Arrogance • Jealousy • Hate • Vanity

Now that you know the four categories of what make up taqwa, you can understand the concept, regardless of what way you choose to refer to it in English. You can also start using the Arabic term "taqwa" regularly instead of using a translation of the term. Since not one translation can capture the entire concept.

You are on your path of Ihsan. What can you work on to increase in Taqwa? Fill in the table.

	Obey the commands	Avoid the prohibitions
Outwardly		
Inwardly		

Protecting One's Outward Requirements (fard)

The Prophet ﷺ relates that Allah said, "My servant does not draw closer to Me by anything more beloved to Me than what I made required (fard) upon him." (Bukhari)

While recommended actions are important for us to develop our Ihsan, our main area of concern is protecting the required parts of our worship and interactions.

As long as we are performing what is required of us, then we can add on recommended acts of devotion. Recommended acts are called sunna, mustahab or nafila.

One way to think about this is to use the language of business. In business, there is capital and then there are profits. Before you can think about making profit, you have to ensure that you are preserving your capital. It would not be good business practice to think that you can make a profit if you are losing your capital. What is required (fard) is your capital. Recommended acts (sunna, mustahab or nafila) are your profits.

Profit: What is recommended

Capital: What is Required

Profit: recommended prayers

Capital: 5 required prayers

Let's take a look at prayer as an example. The most important thing for a Muslim is to preserve the five daily prayers. Those are required (fard) and they are the capital. The recommended prayers before and after them (sunna/nafila) are the profits. The extra prayers in the mid-morning (duha) or before dawn (tahajjud) are also profits.

Any energy that one spends should first be spent on the obligations. If there is energy and ability left over, one can perform extra prayers. One should not spend their limited energy, motivation and time on extra prayers while neglecting the obligatory prayers.

Let's look at an example of an interaction. Respecting, honoring and taking care of one's parents is an obligation (fard). Taking care of friends or random people is a great act, but an extra act.

One should not focus on taking care of friends or strangers while neglecting one's parents.

Profit: taking care of friends and others

Capital: taking care of one's parents

Fill in these circles with the capital and profit of another required and recommended action.

Remembering Allah (Dhikr)

❬Those who believe and whose hearts find comfort in the remembrance of Allah. Surely in the remembrance of Allah do hearts find comfort.❭
Quran 13:28

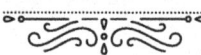

❬And the remembrance of Allah is greater...❭
Quran 29:45

❬And remember Allah abundantly, so that you may be successful❭
Quran 62:10

Remembering Allah (Dhikr) on our tongues is one of the best ways to increase and develop our Ihsan. It purifies our hearts and allows us a fulfilling life and reward in the next life. We should build habits of remembering Allah consistently. The best of actions are the most consistent.

So do as much Dhikr as you can and remember that the best Dhikr is the recitation of the Quran. It is best to read it in Arabic, whether from memory or from the pages of a written copy of the Quran.

There are also many recommended prayers that the Prophet ﷺ taught us to read throughout our day and in different situations. Those are the devotional prayers (dua) and dhikr. These include what to say:

- In the mornings and evenings
- When waking up or going to sleep
- When entering your home or leaving
- Before and after eating
- Before and after using the restroom

There are many, many more devotional prayers (dua) and dhikr that are narrated for specific situations. It is good for the one traveling the path of Ihsan to learn some of these and implement them on a regular basis.

Benefits of dhikr:

- Allah will make mention of you (Quran 2:152)
- It is the greatest action (Quran 29:45)
- There is a great reward in the next life
- It protects you from being from those who lose (Quran 63:9)
- It protects you from the devil (shaytan)
- A way to have your prayers answered
- It will give you a spiritual light

Love of the Prophet ﷺ

The Messenger of Allah ﷺ, said, "None of you have faith until I am more beloved to him than his children, his father, and all of the people." (Bukhari and Muslim)

Love of the Prophet ﷺ is one of the greatest ways to increase our faith and good deeds. We draw closer to Allah the more we love the Prophet ﷺ.

There are many ways to increase our love for the Prophet ﷺ including:

- Reflecting on him and his character ﷺ
- Reading about his life
- Learning about his description
- Reciting poems that praise him

The masjid of the Messenger of Allah ﷺ is in Madinah.

Seeking Knowledge

The Messenger of Allah ﷺ said:

"Seeking knowledge is an obligation upon every Muslim."

and,

"Whoever travels a path in search of knowledge, Allah will make easy for him a path to Paradise. People do not gather in the houses of Allah, reciting the book of Allah and studying it together, but that tranquility will descend upon them, mercy will cover them, angels will surround them, and Allah will mention them to those near Him."

A Muslim must strive to seek knowledge their entire life, from the cradle to the grave. There must be a serious dedication to not do or say anything until we know what the ruling of Allah is concerning that matter. The way we achieve that knowledge is by asking the Muslim scholars or by seeking out the books that they have written for us.

There comes a point where a Muslim goes from passively gaining knowledge, to actively seeking out knowledge. Once a person puts themself in that state, they are a "Seeker of Knowledge". About the Seeker of Knowledge, the Prophet ﷺ said,

"Verily, the angels lower their wings for the seeker of knowledge. The inhabitants of the heavens and earth, even the fish in the depths of the water, seek forgiveness for the scholar. The virtue of the scholar over the worshiper is like the superiority of the moon over the stars. The scholars are the inheritors of the Prophets. They do not leave behind gold or silver coins, but rather they leave behind knowledge. Whoever has taken hold of it has been given an abundant share."

Guarding the Pathways to the Heart

❴**Do not follow what you have no ˹sure˺ knowledge of. Indeed, all will be called to account for ˹their˺ hearing, sight, and intellect.**❵
Quran 17:36

❴**˹O Prophet!˺ Tell the believing men to lower their gaze and guard their chastity. That is purer for them. Surely Allah is All-Aware of what they do. And tell the believing women to lower their gaze and guard their chastity, and not to reveal their adornments except what normally appears.**❵
Quran 24:30-31

Our body is a gift from Allah, and we should use our gifts to serve Him. Our main duty is to use our body to fulfill the obligations and stay away from the prohibitions. Our body parts that we use to obey or disobey are the:

1. Eyes
2. Ears
3. Tongue
4. Hands
5. Feet
6. Stomach
7. Genitals

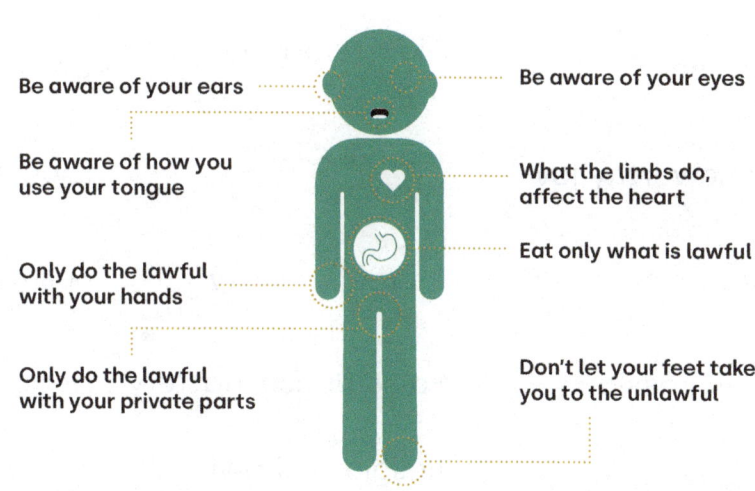

This is an obligation on every single Muslim. The Muslim who is actively trying to be a person of Ihsan will pay even more attention to what these seven do. The path of Ihsan requires that a Muslim not only keep their body parts from falling into what is prohibited, but also to stay far away from the prohibited and also the doubtful matters.

Curing the Diseases of the Heart

{Only those who come before Allah with a pure heart ´will be saved`.}
Quran 26:89

The Messenger of Allah  said, "Verily, in the body is a piece of flesh which, if sound, the entire body is sound, and if corrupt, the entire body is corrupt. Truly, it is the heart."

The heart is the root of all actions. Everything that we do with our limbs began with a thought and feeling in the heart. To change our actions, we have to change our hearts.

The process of purifying the heart consists of two main things:
→ Curing the diseases of the heart
→ Adorning with the stations of Excellence

32 diseases are mentioned in the Quran and Hadith. We must strive to understand the definitions of each and to search our souls to see which of them we have.

We must learn the root causes of each disease as well as the cures. There are cures for each disease once it appears. There are preventative measures we can take to prevent a disease from appearing. You will learn more about this in future Tayba courses. For now, here is a list of 32 of the diseases of the heart that we must work to remove;

Stinginess	Blameworthy shyness	Coveting	Deceit
Blameworthy joy	Blameworthy thoughts	Excessive hope	Boasting
Hate	Fear of poverty	Belief in omens	Arrogance
Transgression	False praise/flattery	Negative opinions	Self-abasement
Love of position	Religious showing off	Vanity	Disdain of criticism
Love of worldly things	Fearing other than God	Cheating	Fear of death
Love of undue praise	Resentment of Divine ordainment	Anger	Discounting blessings
Envy	Religious bragging	Heedlessness	Mockery

Adorning the Heart with the Stations of Excellence

The second part of purifying the heart is adorning ourselves with the stations of excellence. These are all concepts that can be found in the Quran and Hadith. For each station, there are levels that are required and ones that are recommended. You can learn more details about this in IHSN 99 and other Tayba courses.

Name of Station	Definition
Repentance	Repentance that has all conditions fulfilled.
Patience	Patience during trials and with blessings. Also, patience in fulfilling the commands and avoiding the prohibitions.
Gratitude	Using the blessings of Allah in His service.
Fear	Balanced fear that causes one to fulfill the commands and avoid the prohibitions and does not lead to despair.
Hope	Balanced hope that causes one to fulfill the commands and avoid the prohibitions and does not lead to wishful thinking.
Good opinion of Allah	Thinking the best about Allah and His decrees.
Renouncing the World	Having enough detachment from the world to be able to avoid the prohibited matters.
Depending on Allah	Putting in effort while recognizing that Allah is in control.
Acceptance of the Ordainment	Not rejecting what Allah has decreed, inwardly or outwardly. This is the greatest door to reach Allah.
Love	A feeling in the heart that causes one to obey Allah.
Truthfulness	Sincere worship of Allah alone, without any distractions and with full presence.
Sincerity	Sincere worship of Allah, even if there is not full presence.

The 6 M's

Part of the daily practice of the person on the path of Ihsan is to set goals for improvement and work towards them. Then we monitor our thoughts and actions throughout the day and struggle against the self to keep it in line. At the end of the day, we reflect on what we did, didn't do, felt or thought. We weigh all those actions by the scales of Islam: the Quran and Sunnah.

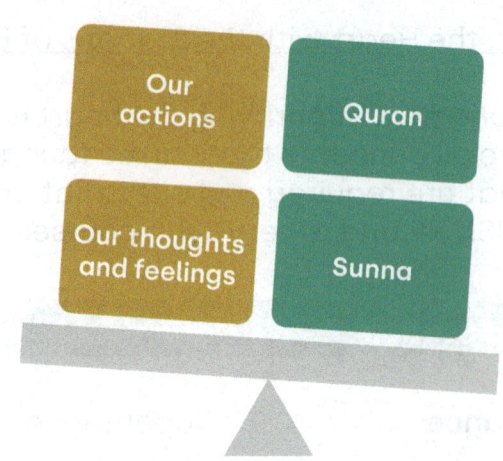

English	Arabic term	How to implement
Goal setting	Musharata	At the beginning of each day, we tell ourselves what goals we want to achieve.
Self-monitoring	Muraqabah	Throughout the day, we keep vigilant watch over our thoughts and actions. Always remembering that Allah sees us.
Exertion/ Struggle	Mujahadah	In fulfilling our goals, we exert force and struggle against the tendencies of our self. This is also known as The Struggle Against the Self. It is referred to as the Greater Struggle.
Self-evaluation	Muhasabah	At the end of the day, before sleeping, we do an accounting of our day. If we achieved our goal, we show gratitude to Allah for granting us the ability to achieve it.
Consequences	Mu'aqabah	If we fall short of a goal, we can reprimand our self. We can take away something (like a treat) that we usually enjoy or reward ourselves with.
Self-reprimand	Mu'atabah	In addition to consequences, we can have self-talk or thoughts to reprimand our self for the goals that were missed.

Choose 3 attainable goals you want to work on for the next while. Write your goals down and then follow the process of the 6 M's every day.

Guides and Fellows

The Prophet ﷺ said, "A person follows the religion of his fellow; so each one should consider whom he makes his fellow."

The Prophet ﷺ said, "The similitude of a good friend and a bad friend is like a perfume-seller and a blacksmith. The perfume-seller might give you perfumes, or you might buy from him, or (at the very least) you might smell its pleasant fragrance. As for the blacksmith, he might burn your clothes, or (at the very least) you will breathe (the fumes') repugnant smell."

As we travel this path of Ihsan, we must realize that we are not alone. We need others to help us in our journey. Allah has created this world in such a way that each of us will have blind spots. There will be things that we may not be able to see about ourselves. We may even benefit and learn something about ourselves from someone who is our enemy.

There will also be knowledge that others hold that we have to seek from them. There may even be things that we know, and we see about ourselves, but we won't make a change until we hear that thing from another person.

These guides and fellows will come in many different forms and fashion. Sometimes, it will be a friend or a family member. Sometimes, the person will be Muslim, and other times they will not. Sometimes it may be a Muslim who does not practice all of Islam. Whatever the state of the person that Allah puts in our path, we must strive to see what wisdom we can gain from that person that will help us in our journey.

The Prophet ﷺ said, "Wisdom is the lost property of the believer. Wherever he finds it, he takes hold of it."

Examples of guides and fellows:

- Good friends
- Family members
- Coaches
- Teachers
- Shaykhs
- Therapists
- Mentors
- Elders

The company we keep will affect us. Reflect on the company you keep. Will it benefit you?

Sincerity

We will end this chapter with a short note on sincerity.

Being sincere means doing something only for Allah. Having a sincere intention is a foundation of our religion. We begin all our acts of worship with an intention.

Before we do anything, we should take a moment to ask ourselves not only if Allah would approve, but if He would be pleased with what we are doing.

A sincere intention is also needed if we want to truly change ourselves and travel on the path of Ihsan. It requires that we think deeply about what we want. If we can get to the point where we are truly sincere about a change we want to make, and we turn to Allah with that sincere intention, Allah will put in our path all that we need to make that change.

> **What are some examples from your life when things were facilitated for you to change once you had a sincere intention to change?**

> **What are some things that you would like to change? Have you reached the point of having a sincere intention to change on those matters?**

True Knowledge of Allah

Once the seeker traveling the path of Ihsan masters all the tools and implements them regularly, that person will become one with true knowledge of Allah. This is a level of knowledge and realization that goes beyond merely knowing about Allah and believing in Him. It is a level of knowledge that causes the person to truly be free and to not have anything else in their heart.

These are the people who Allah has chosen, selected, and made them from among His righteous servants.

May Allah make us from among them.

Developing Ihsan: Tools of the Path

Circle the correct answer.

The Prophet ﷺ compared a good friend to:

a. A blacksmith
b. A carpenter
c. A perfume seller
d. An elder

What should be the center of all our actions?

a. Seeking fame
b. Pleasing family and friends
c. Worshipping Allah
d. Accumulating wealth

What is the station of excellence that involves having a balanced fear of Allah without leading to despair?

a. Hope
b. Fear
c. Patience
d. Sincerity

What is arrogance?

a. Being humble
b. Feeling that one is better than others
c. Feeling sorry for oneself
d. Being overly confident in social settings

Write the term.

_____ : Sincere worship of Allah alone, without any distractions and with full presence

_____ : Goal setting at the beginning of each day in the 6 M's

_____ : Detachment from the world enough to avoid prohibited matters

Why is self-evaluation (Muhasabah) important at the end of the day?

_____

_____

_____

_____

Developing Ihsan: Tools of the Path

Describe a situation where you had to struggle (Mujahadah) against your own desires to meet a goal.

Share an experience where someone helped you see a blind spot in yourself.

What are some of the most important things you learned/reviewed in this chapter?

The Final Hour (As-Sa'a)

MAIN POINTS

- The Final Hour (As-Sa'a) refers to signs that the Last Day/Day of Judgment is near.
- The Final Hour has both minor and major signs.
- Most minor signs are already happening. When major signs happen, it means that the Day of Judgment is about to start.
- The Final Hour (As-Sa'a) is the fourth component of our deen.

LEARNING OBJECTIVES

- To summarize minor and major signs of the Final Hour
- To identify the two signs of the Final Hour mentioned in the Hadith of Jibril

Reflection Questions

- What thoughts and feelings arise when you think about the end of the world?
- Have you ever seen something that made you feel that the End Times are near? What was it?

Key Terms

- **As-Sa'a:** The Final Hour
- **Ummah:** The global Islamic community that includes all the followers of the Prophet Muhammad ﷺ
- **'Isa:** Jesus
- **Dajjal:** The Imposter Christ – his coming will be a great trial. Every prophet warned his people of how difficult it will be. We ask Allah to grant us protection from this test.

Hadith about the Final Hour (As-Sa'a)

From Hadith Jibril:
The man said, "Tell me about the Final Hour **(As-Sa'a)**."
The Messenger ﷺ said, "The one asked knows no more than the one asking."
So, the man said, "Tell me about its signs."
The Messenger ﷺ replied, "The slave-girl will give birth to her mistress, and you will see the barefoot, naked, destitute shepherds compete in the construction of tall buildings." (Bukhari)

<u>Two Signs mentioned in this Hadith</u>

As-Sa'a means the Final Hour. Signs of the Final Hour tell us that the Day of Judgment is near. Knowledge of the signs is the fourth component of our deen.

The Hadith of Jibril tells two signs:

1. "The slave-girl will give birth to her mistress."

Most scholars believe this means that children will act like they are the parents, and the parents are the children. A huge problem in today's society is the disrespect of parents. Basically, the social order will be disrupted. What is abnormal will become normal. You will learn more about the parent-child relationship in your future Tayba course, *Birr99*.

2. "You will see the barefoot, naked, destitute shepherds compete in the construction of tall buildings."

The statement of the Prophet ﷺ has come true. In parts of the Arabian Peninsula, where people once lived as poor sheep and camel herders, they have now become very rich because of oil. There is a rush to build the tallest buildings. This shows that people are competing in advanced technology but are forgetting about their spiritual growth.

How does knowing about the signs of the end of times help you be a better Muslim?

Minor Signs Of the End of Times

The following are more events that will happen as the Last Day approaches, according to hadiths. These statements of the Messenger ﷺ—said over 1400 years ago—are amazingly accurate and relevant to our lifetime.

1   **Loss of trust:**
   This means people no longer trust each other—whether in families, between neighbors, in business, or even between leaders and their supporters.

2   **Widespread fornication and adultery:**
   Today, these actions are often seen as normal. But in reality, it is a type of punishment. These actions bring problems like diseases, children born out of wedlock, and not knowing one's parents.

3   **Widespread acceptance of interest and usury:**
   During the time of the Prophet ﷺ, people of all faiths rarely used interest. Now, it's more common than ever before in history.

4   **Widespread consumption of alcohol:**
   The Prophet ﷺ warned about the increase in alcohol production, advertising, and use. In the past, it was rare in Muslim lands, but today it's very common.

5   **Increase of unnecessary killing:**
   Think of road rage, school shootings, gang violence or military drone attacks that kill innocent people. These are all examples of senseless violence happening today.

6   **Women who are clothed but still naked:**
   Many women wear clothing that is so tight or revealing that it's almost like they're not dressed. This is a trend that has only become common in recent times.

7   **Widespread homosexuality:**
   While homosexuality has always existed, entire societies now embrace and promote it as normal.

8   **Religious knowledge would disappear:**
   People will become more ignorant about their religious responsibilities, and true scholars will become rare.

9   **A man will obey his wife, but disobey his mother; keep friendly relations with his friends, while shunning his father:**
   The Prophet ﷺ briefly described how people would disrespect their parents but still maintain ties with their friends, showing the decline in family values.

10 **Great distances will be travelled in a short time:**
The Prophet ﷺ foretold of a time when people would be able to travel far in a short amount of time. We see this now in the form of modern transportation, like airplanes, trains, and cars which allow people to travel far distances in just a short amount of time.

Less than 200 years ago, it would take about a month to travel from New York to California using a steam ship and the railroad. Today, the average flight between these two states is about 6 hours.

Circle the number next to the minor sign that you have seen in your own life.

Major Signs of the End Times

These major signs mentioned by the Messenger ﷺ announce that Judgment Day is about to happen. These events will occur quickly one after another, falling like the beads of a broken necklace. They are not in order:

- The coming of Imam Mahdi:
  A direct descendant of the Messenger ﷺ who will come in a time of upheaval and confusion for the Muslims. He will help the global Islamic community **(ummah)** improve its dire situation.

- The return of the Prophet Jesus **('Isa)**:
  The Prophet Jesus ('Isa) will return to earth to complete his mission, which will include teaching the truth of his servanthood to Allah and supporting the Shari'a (sacred law) of Prophet Muhammad ﷺ.

- The appearance of the **Dajjal** (imposter Christ):
  A great liar will appear who will claim to be a prophet and then claim divinity. He will be given powers by which to test the faith of people. He will be able to travel the earth swiftly, causing havoc wherever he goes. He will finally be confronted and killed by the Prophet Jesus. Believers will know who he is.

- The appearance of Gog and Magog:
  An uncivilized tribe of people will emerge from a place on earth and will cause killing and bloodshed wherever they go until they are caused to die, after which the earth is cleansed of them.

- The rising of the Beast from the earth:
  A beast will arise from the earth who will communicate with humans, confirming the truth of the messengers, and who will be able to differentiate between believers and unbelievers.

- The spread of smoke over the earth:
  This smoke will be harmful to mankind and will spread all over the earth affecting believers lightly and non-believers greatly.

- The rising of the sun from the west:
  Right before the Day of Judgment, the sun will rise from the west, at which time no more repentance will be accepted from humankind. This is the last major sign that will announce the End of Time.

Important Reminder

It's important for Muslims to remember the End Times because of the difficulties that these times will bring. There will be massive social, psychological and religious upheaval as Judgment Day approaches. It can be faith-shaking if you do not know that all of these things were foretold by the final Messenger ﷺ.

As Muslims, we should not do anything to try to speed up these signs. They are all under the control and timeline of Allah. However, we also do our best to keep away from the actions of the people mentioned in these signs. Even if we do not live to witness the End of Time, our accountability begins when we die.

The Final Hour (As-Sa'a)

Use the clues to find and circle the answers in the puzzle. Then write the answers on the line. Answers can be down, across, or diagonal.

Z	T	X	U	D	A	J	J	A	L
O	I	P	S	M	J	J	Z	L	L
P	Q	X	I	M	M	F	A	U	N
E	D	W	G	C	X	A	M	M	B
D	K	D	N	U	C	U	H	A	C
N	J	M	S	S	C	X	W	H	M
I	N	T	E	R	E	S	T	D	J
Z	B	E	J	O	V	C	H	I	J
U	L	L	T	K	C	H	T	H	G
F	V	Y	K	E	R	U	C	B	M

_____means the global Islamic community.

_____ is the name of the great liar who will appear near the end of times.

Major and minor _____ tell us about the End of Time.

This is very common today but is forbidden in Islam, and is related to money lending:

_____

Imam _____ is a descendant of the Prophet ﷺ who will come to help the Muslim community.

The Final Hour (As-Sa'a)

Why do you think it's important to learn about the signs of the End Times?

Which sign of the End Times stood out to you the most, and why?

What are some of the most important things you learned/reviewed in this chapter?

This is an optional section.
Completing it is not necessary for the successful completion of this book.

Masjids Around the World – Art Therapy

Copy/draw, decorate or color this masjid while learning about it.

Kul Sharif Mosque, Russia

The Kul Sharif Mosque, originally built in the Kazan Kremlin in the 16th century was named after the scholar Kul Sharif. It was destroyed during the Siege of Kazan in 1552 by Ivan the Terrible's forces. A new mosque was built in its place and completed in 2005.

Marriage in Islam, and the High Status of Women

MAIN POINTS

- Marriage is an important part of Islam and should increase both the husband and wife in faith and good deeds.
- Marriage should be very carefully considered before being entered into.
- A Muslim should delay marriage until they know they can fulfill the rights of their wife or husband.
- Women have a high status in Islam, the same as men.
- Islam gives women many rights, including financial, marital, and social.
- The best of men are those who treat their wives well.

LEARNING OBJECTIVES

- To understand what makes a beneficial marriage
- To explain the rights of spouses and children in Islam
- To appreciate the high status of women in Islam
- To clear up common misconceptions regarding marriage and women

Reflection Questions

- If you are married, what is the best way to keep good ties with your spouse from prison?
- If you are not married, what are some qualities you can work on that will make you a good husband/wife in the future?

Key Terms

- **Nikah:** An Islamic marriage ceremony
- **Wali:** A trustworthy Muslim male representative that protects the interests of the bride
- **Mahr:** obligatory marriage gift

Marriage in Islam

❴ And one of His signs is that He created for you spouses from among yourselves so that you may find comfort in them. And He has placed between you compassion and mercy. Surely in this are signs for people who reflect. ❵

Quran 30:21

Marriage is important in Islam and a good marriage is a huge blessing. The Prophet ﷺ stated that marriage is "half of religion" (Taqwa is the second half). Marriage should be beneficial for both the husband and wife.

Marriage must be very carefully considered since it involves the rights of another person. In some situations, getting married may even be sinful (haram).

You must ensure your marriage is both valid and pleasing to Allah. If you cannot, it is better to remain single than enter into a marriage where either you or your spouse will be harmed.

An Islamic marriage ceremony is called a **nikah**.

Preparing for a Nikah

To have a nikah done you must have:

People	Item
› A groom	› A gift for the bride
› A bride	
› The bride's male representative (wali)	
› At least two male witnesses	

The bride should have a **wali** (male representative) to represent her interests. The wali is usually a male relative from the wife's family, but he can also be the imam or a trustworthy Muslim man.

The marriage gift for the bride, called **mahr**, should be decided on before the nikah. The imam performing the nikah should be informed about the mahr. The bride's wali should be present.

The gift (mahr) is often a ring, money, or both.

<u>The Process of Nikah</u>

The couple would go to an imam or to a masjid.

It is recommended (sunnah) for the imam to first give a sermon (khutbah) about marriage. Then:

the Imam will ask the wali if he agrees to the bride's marriage to the groom, for the stated mahr. If the wali agrees	the imam then asks the groom if he agrees to marry the bride. If the groom agrees,	the imam says a dua to bless the marriage.

The marriage is now complete.

Rights of Spouses and Children

It's necessary for spouses to fulfill each other's rights.

Husbands are responsible for:	A wife's responsibilities are:
providing basic necessities for their wives and children. These include: shelter, food, clothing, and health needs. Husbands should treat their wives with kindness, respect and patience.	to respect her husband as the leader of the family (as long as Islamic teachings are followed) and to treat her husband with kindness, respect and patience.

<u>Physical Intimacy & Marriage:</u>

- An Islamic marriage protects both husband and wife from committing adultery.
- Both spouses in a marriage have a right to have their intimate physical needs fulfilled by the other.
- In the case where there is physical separation due to travel or incarceration, the other spouse can give up this right if they choose.
- A spouse has grounds to ask for an Islamic divorce based on lack of intimacy.
- If lack of physical intimacy is causing one spouse to fear falling into the prohibited with someone else, then it may be better to separate through a divorce, and for that spouse to marry someone who can fulfill their needs.
- In such cases, before seeking a divorce, a Muslim should try to remedy the marriage if at all possible. This can be through counseling, therapy, or seeking advice from trusted people.

The Prophet ﷺ said:

"When a Muslim spends something on his family, intending to receive the reward of Allah, it is regarded as charity for him." (Bukhari)

<u>Before Considering Marriage</u>

Men must ensure that they can provide for a wife. Both men and women should ensure they are ready to put another person first and to always treat them kindly and with respect.

It is preferred in Islam for men to marry Muslim women. However, if a man is married to a Christian woman, she has the same rights as a Muslim wife. The husband should kindly encourage her to accept Islam. If she does not choose to accept Islam, it is required that the children be raised as Muslims.

Children also have rights in Islam. In addition to having all their material needs provided for by their father, children have the following rights:

- To be given a good upbringing and education
- To be treated fairly with their siblings
- To be given a good name

The rules of marriage (and divorce) will be discussed more in future Tayba courses.

The High Status of Women in Islam

Muslim women have a high status with Allah, our Lord and Creator. Regardless of how women may be viewed by society, know that this is only temporary, and Muslim women are highly honored and respected.

Over 1,400 years ago, when most civilizations viewed women as property without rights, the Prophet Muhammad ﷺ taught that women have rights given by Allah. Some of these rights include:

1. Equality

There is no difference between women and men spiritually. They both can earn reward with their Creator equally. Allah tells us in the Quran:

> ❰**Muslim men and Muslim women, believing men and believing women, obedient men and obedient women, truthful men and truthful women, patient men and patient women, humble men and humble women, charitable men and charitable women, fasting men and fasting women, men who guard their chastity and women who guard, men who remember Allah frequently and women who remember—Allah has prepared for them pardon, and a magnificent reward.**❱
> **Quran 33:35**

The Messenger ﷺ said, "Verily, women are the counterparts of men." (Sahih Tirmidhi)

2. Financial Rights

One of the greatest rights of people is to earn and spend their money as they choose. Allah made it clear that both men and women have a right to what they own.

⟨...For men is a share of what they have earned, and for women is a share of what they have earned...⟩
Quran 4:32

A Muslim woman can work and keep all that she earns, even if she is wealthy and has a husband who is poor. A woman's money or property does not transfer over to the control of the husband at the time of marriage.

⟨ Men receive a share of what their parents and relatives leave, and women receive a share of what their parents and relatives leave; be it little or much—a legal share.⟩
Quran 4:7

Islam also gave women the right to inheritance at a time when most societies denied them this right.

3. Rank of Mothers and Wives

Concerning wives, the Prophet of Allah ﷺ said:

"The most complete of believers in faith are those with the best character. And the best of you are the best in behavior to their women." (Sahih Tirmidhi)

About mothers he ﷺ said, "Paradise is at the feet of the mothers." (Sahih Nasa'i)

"He ﷺ was once asked by a man, 'Who is most deserving of my good company?' The Messenger ﷺ replied: 'Your mother.' The man asked, 'Then who?' He ﷺ again said, 'Your mother.' The man asked again, 'Then who?' Again he ﷺ replied, 'Your mother.' The man asked again, 'Then who?' Only then did he ﷺ say, 'Your father'." (Bukhari and Muslim)

4. Freedom to Choose a Husband

A Muslim woman can choose who she marries. She is free to either accept or reject a marriage proposal, or she may propose to a Muslim man herself.

Although she has the choice, marriage is never something that should be entered into lightly. One needs to be cautious and smart about when and who one marries. Take the advice of people who care about you and are in a position to give good advice.

5. Female Role Models

There are many strong Muslim women role models. From the beginning of Islam, Khadija, the wife of the Prophet Muhammad ﷺ, believed in him and supported him in every way until she passed away.

Women have a special ability to love deeply. All these great women share a strong love for Allah and His Mesenger ﷺ. Through this love and faith, they found patience, kindness, and strength.

One of the greatest scholars was Aisha bint Abi Bakr. She was the wife of the Prophet ﷺ after Khadija's passing. She learned from the Prophet ﷺ for 10 years, memorizing his words and actions. After he ﷺ passed away, she spent nearly 50 years teaching others. If male Companions of the Prophet ﷺ disagreed on something, they would ask Aisha for her opinion.

Thanks to her, thousands of hadiths are still preserved today. She didn't just narrate hadiths, but she also explained their meanings.

A woman's quiet life of serving her family and engaging in private worship can be as meaningful as public roles in the community. Success, often tied to careers and education, doesn't define one's worth with Allah, who values sincerity and the heart over status or wealth.

6. No Violence Against Women

In Islam, men are the protectors of women. Men are to stand up for women's religious rights and shield them from harm. It should, therefore, go without saying that it is absolutely prohibited in Islam to beat a woman, whether a wife, daughter or anyone else. Such a sinful action goes directly against the very teachings of the religion.

If you have grown up believing otherwise you must do your best to rid yourself of such beliefs and remind yourself of the gravity of this sin. This is a direct commandment from the Prophet ﷺ: "Never beat the women servants of Allah." (Abu Dawud)

Marital abuse of any kind is strictly forbidden. Allah says:

❨...do not retain them ˹only˺ to harm them ˹or˺ to take advantage ˹of them˺. Whoever does that surely wrongs his own soul. Do not take Allah's revelations lightly.❩
Quran 2:231

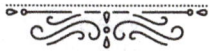

The Prophet Muhammad ﷺ never hit a woman, as reported by his own wife Aisha: "The Messenger of Allah never struck a servant with his hand, nor did he ever hit a woman." (Muslim)

In fact, the Prophet ﷺ tied a man's honor to how well he treats his wife:

"The honorable man treats women with respect, and the despicable one treats women poorly," and "the best of you are those who are best to their wives and families." (Tirmidhi)

Quran verse 4:34, which some misinterpret as Islam allowing wife-beating, is referring to a harmless tap with a toothbrush or handkerchief, to symbolize the seriousness of a marital problem.

Any man who comes close to the sinful action of abusing others should seek help. Any woman who is being abused should not continue to endure it in the name of having patience. One must protect themselves – this can mean marriage counseling or immediately seeking safety by removing oneself and one's children from the situation.

Modesty

Both men and women are rewarded for modesty in Islam. It is an internal good trait that usually develops over time. Beginning with being modest outwardly leads to becoming modest inwardly.

Modesty helps protect us from societal harms.

Type	When?	Women	Men
Outward Physical Modesty	Around non-family members of the opposite gender	› Wearing loose fitting clothing that covers all skin aside from face and hands (and some scholars allow feet). › Wearing a headscarf (hijab).	› Wearing loose fitting upper garments that cover the upper arms, shoulders, chest, and lower garments that cover down past the knees. › Covering one's head, such as with a hat or kufi. › Growing a tidy beard.
Inward Modesty of Character	At all times for both genders	› Not acting arrogantly with any person › Not boasting, especially about sinful things › Not being flirtatious or overly friendly with the opposite gender	

Some people have false ideas about women and modesty in Islam. The following points are NOT true:

✗ Women must wear black whenever leaving the house
✗ Women should be physically forced to wear a headscarf
✗ Women cannot work outside of the home

Marriage in Islam, and the High Status of Women

1. Write 3 specific rights that Islam gives to women.

2. What are the responsibilities of a husband in an Islamic marriage?

3. What are the responsibilities of a wife in an Islamic marriage?

Write (T) for True and (F) for False.

1		Men and women are not spiritually equal.
2		A daughter must accept the spouse that her parents choose for her.
3		The Prophet Muhammad ﷺ forbade men from beating women, and he ﷺ never struck a woman.
4		Christian wives do not have the same rights as Muslim wives in a marriage.
5		Aisha, a wife of the Messenger ﷺ, was a great scholar of Islam.

Marriage in Islam, and the High Status of Women

Why might some Muslims not follow Islam's teachings about women?

Why do you think Islam has rules for the rights of spouses and children in marriage?

What are some of the most important things you learned/reviewed in this chapter?

This is an optional section.
Completing it is not necessary for the successful completion of this book.

Masjids Around the World – Art Therapy

Copy/draw, decorate or color this masjid while learning about it.

Al-Azhar Mosque, Egypt

Al-Azhar Mosque in Cairo, Egypt, was founded in 970 by the Fatimid Caliphate and became the first mosque in the city. It later grew into a major center of Islamic learning. Al-Azhar University, connected to the mosque, is one of the oldest in the world and is renowned for its study of Islamic theology and law. Despite periods of neglect, it was revitalized, especially under the Mamluks, and remains a highly influential Islamic institution today.

Islam 98 Answer Key

CHAPTER 1

Introduction to Islam

1. What is the Quran?
The Quran is the final revelation from Allah. It is the words of Allah.

2. What is the Sunnah?
The Sunnah is preserved narrations of everything the Prophet Muhammed, peace be upon him, said, did, or affirmed.

Circle True or False.

1. We submit to Allah by doing what pleases Him. **True** / False
2. We don't have to follow the Sunnah. True / **False**
3. Islam is a life-long journey. **True** / False
4. All prophets taught their followers to submit to Allah. **True** / False

There are 4 components of this Deen. Which component is this from?

Islam	:	prayer
Islam	:	fasting
Islam	:	belief in the angels
Iman	:	to worship Allah as if you see Him
Signs of As-Sa'a	:	The barefoot, naked, destitute shepherds will compete in the construction of tall buildings.

CHAPTER 2

The 5 Pillars of Islam

Write the name of the pillar of islam.

Shahada	:	a phrase you declare to let others know you are Muslim.
Prayer	:	Muslims do this five times a day.
Fasting	:	Muslims do this in the month of Ramadan.

Circle True or False.

1. Once a person makes a statement of faith in Islam, we should investigate and figure out if that person is indeed a Muslim. True / **False**
2. If a person says that he/she is a Muslim, that is enough for us to treat them as Muslim and offer them all the rights they are owed. **True** / False
3. If a person believes exactly what Muslims believe, but has not formally spoken the shahada, he or she is still considered to be Muslim with Allah. **True** / False
4. If a person says the shahada without understanding the words or believing the meaning, he or she is still considered to be a Muslim by Allah. True / **False**
5. The shahada can be said in any language, and it can be done in any place. **True** / False
6. A Muslim who struggles with their 5 daily prayers is no longer a Muslim. True / **False**

Why is it important for a person to not delay in saying their shahada?
A person may pass away before announcing their belief. Asking a person to delay the Shahada is like saying, "You should remain in disbelief for a little longer"

CHAPTER 3

Preparation for Prayer (Salah)

Write 3 things one can do to prepare for prayer. *Answers may vary but may include:*

1. Washing off physical impurities from body, clothing, and place of prayer.
2. Performing wudu.
3. Freeing the heart and mind from anything other than Allah and His Messenger, peace be upon him.

List 2 differences between wudu and ghusl. *Answers may vary but may include:*

Wudu is done on specific limbs but ghusl requires washing the whole body.

The causes for wudu are different than the causes for ghusl.

Circle True or False.

1. One can do tayammum if water is too expensive. **True** / False
2. One wipes their feet with soil in tayammum. True / **False**
3. Wudu is often done multiple times a day. **True** / False
4. Falling asleep invalidates tayammum. **True** / False
5. Tayammum done to replace wudu or ghusl is done in the same way for both. **True** / False
6. If you don't have enough water for ghusl, make wudu instead. True / **False**

What is the main purpose of prayer?
The main purpose of prayer is to fill our hearts with an awareness of the greatness of Allah. It also helps us to gain the pleasure and Mercy of Allah.

CHAPTER 4

Performing Prayer (Salah)

Fill in the table.

Prayer	Time of Day	Number of Cycles
Fajr	Dawn	2
Dhuhr	Midday	4
Asr	Late Afternoon	4
Maghrib	Sunset	3
Isha	Night	4

Write the correct word.

Al-Fatiha	:	This chapter of the Quran is recited in every cycle.
Prostration	:	Do this action twice in each cycle. Sit in between both.
Allahu Akbar	:	Make your intention then say this to begin your prayer.
The Abrahamic Greeting	:	This greeting is only read in the final seating of prayer.

Write two of each.

Things you need to do before prayer to prepare for it:

1. Answers will vary
2. Answers will vary

Things that invalidate the prayer:

1. Answers will vary
2. Answers will vary

Answers may vary for the questions that require personal reflection.
Answers given here may not be the only correct answer.

Islam 98 Answer Key

CHAPTER 5

Other Prayer Topics + Zakah

Circle the correct answer.

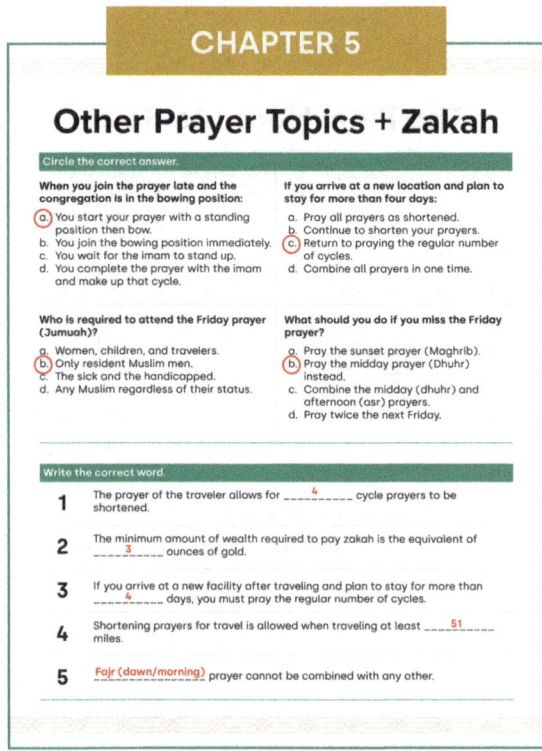

When you join the prayer late and the congregation is in the bowing position:
- **a.** You start your prayer with a standing position then bow.
- b. You join the bowing position immediately.
- c. You wait for the imam to stand up.
- d. You complete the prayer with the imam and make up that cycle.

If you arrive at a new location and plan to stay for more than four days:
- a. Pray all prayers as shortened.
- b. Continue to shorten your prayers.
- **c.** Return to praying the regular number of cycles.
- d. Combine all prayers in one time.

Who is required to attend the Friday prayer (Jumuah)?
- a. Women, children, and travelers.
- **b.** Only resident Muslim men.
- c. The sick and the handicapped.
- d. Any Muslim regardless of their status.

What should you do if you miss the Friday prayer?
- a. Pray the sunset prayer (Maghrib).
- **b.** Pray the midday prayer (Dhuhr) instead.
- c. Combine the midday (dhuhr) and afternoon (asr) prayers.
- d. Pray twice the next Friday.

Write the correct word.

1. The prayer of the traveler allows for _____**4**_____ cycle prayers to be shortened.

2. The minimum amount of wealth required to pay zakah is the equivalent of _____**3**_____ ounces of gold.

3. If you arrive at a new facility after traveling and plan to stay for more than _____**4**_____ days, you must pray the regular number of cycles.

4. Shortening prayers for travel is allowed when traveling at least _____**51**_____ miles.

5. _____**Fajr (dawn/morning)**_____ prayer cannot be combined with any other.

CHAPTER 6

Fasting in Ramadan

Answers may vary but may include:
Write two benefits of fasting.

1. It helps us avoid doing wrong.

2. It teaches us to be more kind and caring towards people in poverty.

Write (T) for True and (F) for False.

1. **T** Ramadan is the month in which the Quran was first revealed.

2. **T** Good deeds are given greater weight in Ramadan.

3. **F** Fasting starts at Dhuhr prayer and ends at Isha prayer.

4. **F** Muslims are encouraged to fast only in Ramadan.

5. **T** If a person forgetfully eats or drinks something while fasting, their fast is still valid and they should continue the fast.

6. **F** Eid al-Fitr begins on the last day of Ramadan.

Answers may vary but may include:
Write 2 situations where fasting during Ramadan is not required.

1. A person who cannot fast due to chronic illness.

2. A traveler

What should a Muslim do if they intentionally break their fast to smoke?
This person should make up the day and repent for what they did.

CHAPTER 7

The Six Pillars of Belief

What are the 6 Pillars of Belief in Islam?
The 6 Pillars of Belief are believing in Allah, His Angels, His revealed Books, His Messengers, the Last Day, and predestination.

Write (T) for True and (F) for False.

1. **T** The most important belief of Islam is the Oneness of Allah.

2. **F** Angels are made of white clay.

3. **T** Angels always obey Allah.

4. **F** Satan is a fallen angel.

5. **T** There will be no more prophets or messengers after the Prophet Muhammad ﷺ.

6. **T** Today's Bible contains untrue stories of prophets.

Name 3 angels and their assigned role:

1. Answers will vary.

2. Answers will vary.

3. Answers will vary.

Name 2 necessary characteristics of prophets and messengers.

1. Truthfulness

2. Trustworthiness

CHAPTER 8

Excellence (Ihsan)

In your own words, describe Ihsan.
Answers will vary.

Write down some ideas on how you can increase in Ihsan in your life.
Answers will vary.

What are the 2 levels of Ihsan?
1. To worship Allah as if you can see Him.
2. To worship Allah knowing He sees you.

Write (T) for True and (F) for False.

1. **T** Ihsan means trying to please Allah in everything we do—what we think, feel, do, or avoid doing.

2. **F** Ihsan only applies to acts of worship.

3. **T** You can, and should, have Ihsan in your interactions with others.

4. **T** The Prophet Muhammad ﷺ said that whoever believes in Allah and the Last Day should have excellence (Ihsan) with their neighbor.

5. **T** Worshiping Allah with Ihsan means you worship as if you can see Him, and if you don't see Him, knowing He sees you.

Answers may vary for the questions that require personal reflection.
Answers given here may not be the only correct answer.

Islam 98 Answer Key

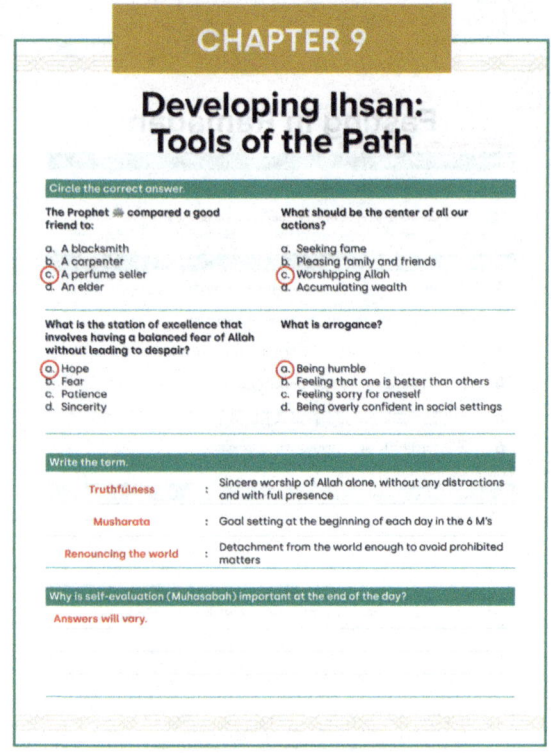

CHAPTER 9

Developing Ihsan: Tools of the Path

Circle the correct answer.

The Prophet ﷺ compared a good friend to:
a. A blacksmith
b. A carpenter
c. A perfume seller
d. An elder

What should be the center of all our actions?
a. Seeking fame
b. Pleasing family and friends
c. Worshipping Allah
d. Accumulating wealth

What is the station of excellence that involves having a balanced fear of Allah without leading to despair?
a. Hope
b. Fear
c. Patience
d. Sincerity

What is arrogance?
a. Being humble
b. Feeling that one is better than others
c. Feeling sorry for oneself
d. Being overly confident in social settings

Write the term.

Truthfulness	: Sincere worship of Allah alone, without any distractions and with full presence
Musharata	: Goal setting at the beginning of each day in the 6 M's
Renouncing the world	: Detachment from the world enough to avoid prohibited matters

Why is self-evaluation (Muhasabah) important at the end of the day?

Answers will vary.

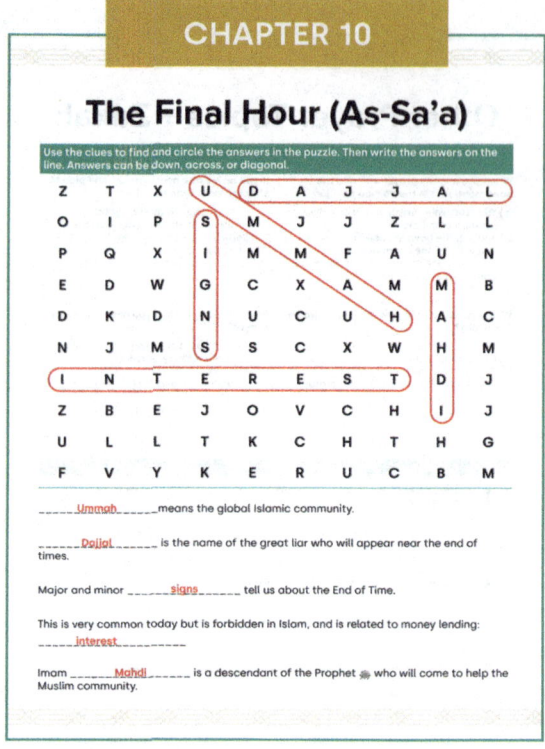

CHAPTER 10

The Final Hour (As-Sa'a)

Use the clues to find and circle the answers in the puzzle. Then write the answers on the line. Answers can be down, across, or diagonal.

Z	T	X	U	D	A	J	J	A	L
O	I	P	S	M	J	J	Z	L	L
P	Q	X	I	M	M	F	A	U	N
E	D	W	G	C	X	A	M	M	B
D	K	D	N	U	C	U	H	A	C
N	J	M	S	S	C	X	W	H	M
I	N	T	E	R	E	S	T	D	J
Z	B	E	J	O	V	C	H	I	J
U	L	L	T	K	C	H	T	H	G
F	V	Y	K	E	R	U	C	B	M

_____Ummah_____ means the global Islamic community.

_____Dajjal_____ is the name of the great liar who will appear near the end of times.

Major and minor _____signs_____ tell us about the End of Time.

This is very common today but is forbidden in Islam, and is related to money lending: _____interest_____

Imam _____Mahdi_____ is a descendant of the Prophet ﷺ who will come to help the Muslim community.

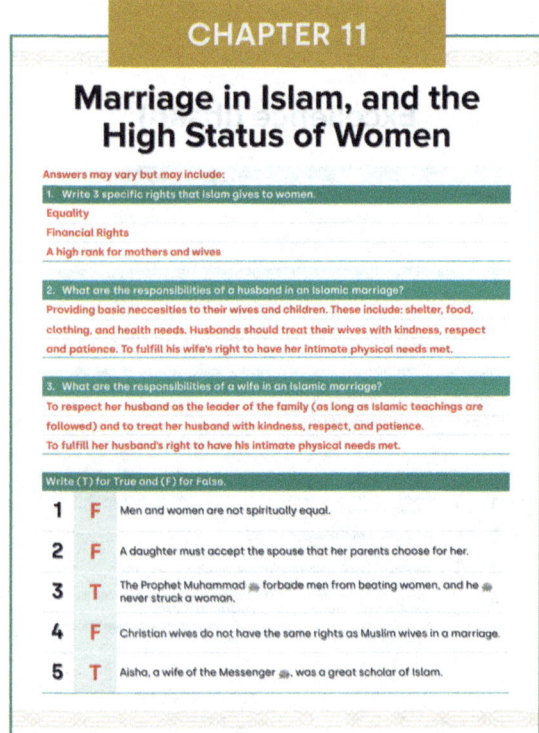

CHAPTER 11

Marriage in Islam, and the High Status of Women

Answers may vary but may include:

1. Write 3 specific rights that Islam gives to women.
Equality
Financial Rights
A high rank for mothers and wives

2. What are the responsibilities of a husband in an Islamic marriage?
Providing basic necessities to their wives and children. These include: shelter, food, clothing, and health needs. Husbands should treat their wives with kindness, respect and patience. To fulfill his wife's right to have her intimate physical needs met.

3. What are the responsibilities of a wife in an Islamic marriage?
To respect her husband as the leader of the family (as long as Islamic teachings are followed) and to treat her husband with kindness, respect, and patience.
To fulfill her husband's right to have his intimate physical needs met.

Write (T) for True and (F) for False.

1. **F** Men and women are not spiritually equal.

2. **F** A daughter must accept the spouse that her parents choose for her.

3. **T** The Prophet Muhammad ﷺ forbade men from beating women, and he ﷺ never struck a woman.

4. **F** Christian wives do not have the same rights as Muslim wives in a marriage.

5. **T** Aisha, a wife of the Messenger ﷺ, was a great scholar of Islam.

Answers may vary for the questions that require personal reflection.
Answers given here may not be the only correct answer.

Mail back to Tayba.

Islam 98 - End Reflection

Name: _____

ID Number: _____

End-of-Book checklist:
Please check off each box to confirm that you've completed the text.

☐ All the review sections are complete at the end of each chapter.

☐ All the reflection questions are answered to the best of my ability.

☐ I have checked all the section reviews with the answer key at the end of the textbook.

☐ I have reviewed all the incorrect answers and understand where my mistakes in the answers were. If I don't understand why my answer was wrong, I will write Tayba and ask.

Choose any 3 reflection questions from the book that were meaningful to you.
Copy your answers down here.

1. Chapter Number: _____   Question Number: _____

_____
_____
_____
_____
_____
_____
_____
_____
_____
_____

Mail back to Tayba.

Islam 98 - End Reflection

Name: _____

ID Number: _____

2. Chapter Number: _____ Question Number: _____

_____

_____

_____

_____

_____

_____

_____

_____

_____

_____

3. Chapter Number: _____ Question Number: _____

_____

_____

_____

_____

_____

_____

_____

_____

_____

Mail back to Tayba.

Mail back to Tayba.

Islam 98 - End Reflection

Name: _____

ID Number: _____

Write down any questions that you have about the topics in this text that have not been answered.

_____

_____

_____

_____

_____

_____

_____

_____

_____

_____

Write a short summary telling us some of the most notable things to you, that you learned in this book. You may want to refer back to the last reflection question in each chapter.

_____

_____

_____

_____

_____

_____

_____

_____

_____

Mail back to Tayba.

Islam 98 - End Reflection

Name: _____

ID Number: _____

TAYBA FOUNDATION
Freedom Through Education

TAYBA FOUNDATION CORRESPONDENCE PROGRAMS APPLICATION
PLEASE WRITE CLEARLY IN INK (NO PENCIL) AND SIGN TO AVOID DELAYS IN YOUR ADMISSION PROCESS

Full legal name: _____   Preferred name (if applicable): _____

Prison ID No: _____   Birth Date (MM/DD/YYYY): _____

Institution Name: _____   Institution type: [ ] Federal [ ] State [ ] County

Institution Address: _____

Dorm/Unit #: _____   City: _____   State: _____   Zip Code: _____

Expected Parole (MM/DD/YYYY): _____   Expected Release Date (MM/DD/YYYY): _____

Check if you have access to: [ ] Phone [ ] Tablet [ ] Email (Please identify: *Ex:* JPay, Corrlinks, *etc.*)

> *Note that for those of you who have access to Corrlinks and some who have JPay, you will need to add instructors@taybafoundation.org to your contacts list before we can add you to our contacts.*

I am interested in taking courses in: [ ] Islamic Studies   [ ] Life Skills [ ] Both

Please note that it is extremely important for you to keep us updated with any changes in your address/unit, etc. so we can ensure your books and course materials are sent to the correct address. It is your responsibility to ensure that the mailroom can/will accept mail/shipments from Tayba Foundation.

By signing and submitting this application form, you are agreeing to participate in the entire Tayba Curriculum, or as much of the curriculum as possible, in the order set out by Tayba. As Tayba adds new courses and/or changes existing courses, Tayba reserves the right to update the order of the curriculum path. By signing and submitting this application form, you are authorizing Tayba Foundation to accept and use financial aid available on your behalf to cover the monthly cost of your subscription. Full details of Tayba's Financial Aid Policy found on the following page. Please review before signing. By signing and submitting this application form, you are agreeing to abide by the Guidelines for Students that was sent with this application.

By my signature below, I acknowledge and accept Tayba Foundation's Financial Aid Policy and Guidelines for Students. I certify that the information contained in this application form is true and complete.

Signature of Student: _____   *Date:* _____

Supplementary Student information that will help us serve you better:

The following five items **(A - E)** will not affect your admission in any way. This data assists Tayba Foundation in applying for grants to continue offering our services at low or no cost to our student population.

A. [ ] Raised Muslim [ ] Converted in prison [ ] Converted in Society

B. Years as a Muslim (if converted): _____

C. Gender: [ ] Male [ ] Female

wwD. Ethnicity (optional): _____

E. Highest level of education:
[ ] Some high school [ ] High school [ ] GED [ ] Some College [ ] AA [ ] BA/BS [ ] MS [ ] PhD

Section regarding Facility Approval:

I, [name and title] _____, have completed the necessary paperwork required by my facility to participate in Correspondence Courses with Tayba Foundation. I have confirmed that I have permission to receive Tayba coursebooks, correspondence, and any additional educational resource materials required to complete my course(s).

If your Educational Director or Chaplain has any questions about our organization or our correspondence program, they can contact Lumumba K. Shakur, Lead Instructor at instructors@taybafoundation.org or by phone at 510-491-7859.

NOTE: If you receive your mail in digital format only, you can send us an email message with the following message: "I, [your first and last name and prison ID], have read the entirety of the TAYBA FOUNDATION Financial Aid Policy and I accept these terms and conditions. I have completed the necessary paperwork required by my facility to participate in Correspondence Courses with Tayba Foundation and I have confirmed that I have permission to receive Tayba coursebooks, correspondence, and any additional educational resource materials required to complete my course(s)."

TAYBA FOUNDATION FINANCIAL AID POLICY

Financial Aid Policy: Tuition with Tayba Foundation's distance learning programs and access to Tayba Foundation services costs $100 (one hundred) dollars per month. To date, we have been successful in finding financial aid for all our students. By submitting this form, you are authorizing Tayba Foundation to accept and use financial aid available on your behalf to cover this monthly cost. **No cash will be sent to you.** The monthly subscription cost will include, but is not limited to, books and other relevant educational resources, as well as shipping costs and sales tax. This will also allow access to any newsletters you sign up for, Life Skills courses, our Reentry coaching and planning, and our peer mentor services. Tayba receives grants and donations for our program from a number of sources. If you choose not to use Tayba's financial aid, please enclose a check or money order to cover the cost of $100.00 (one hundred) dollars per month.

f you wish to cancel your access at any time, please submit your notice to Tayba Foundation in writing. If we do not receive any communication from you for a period of twelve (12) months, we will consider you "inactive." If any communications Tayba sends you is returned to us (Return To Sender - RTS), we will attempt to resend. If we are not able to send to a new address, we will consider your subscription inactive. Should you become inactive in distance learning programs or other Tayba Foundation services, your access will be put on hold and Tayba Foundation will cease to collect the $100 per month financial aid on your behalf. You can reactivate your subscription to Tayba Foundation's services by mail, email or phone, letting us know that you would still like to be on our mailing list and remain eligible for our educational programs and other services. Note that Tayba Foundation's distance learning programs follow a set learning schedule of semesters. Tayba Foundation's services are not unlimited. However, we have been able to accommodate all reasonable requests for services to date.

If you wish to cancel your access at any time, please submit your notice to Tayba Foundation in writing. If we do not receive any communication from you for a period of twelve (12) months, we will consider you "inactive."

TAYBA FOUNDATION GUIDELINES FOR STUDENTS

The superiority of knowledge has been clearly established through the Qur'ān and the sayings of the Prophet Muhammad ﷺ. Those that aid in the pursuit of knowledge are given a great reward. So, it is an honor for our organization to facilitate education for those who are seekers of knowledge. To ensure that the education process remains unhindered for our students, teachers and the organization, we expect all those who participate in the Distance Learning Program to understand and abide by these guidelines. Failure to comply with these guidelines will result in expulsion from the Distance Learning Program.

1. **Education is our goal and security is our primary concern.**
   a. Students must fully comply with prison regulations and protocols at all times.
   b. No material of the Tayba Foundation shall be used by students to legitimize otherwise illegal activity.
   c. Adherence to the laws of the land is a duty on all. Our obedience to established laws comes from our obedience to our Lord. All students will be expected to obey the laws and not do anything to circumvent said laws.
   d. No student shall be engaged in any illegal activity. We have a zero-tolerance policy in this regard.
   e. In those cases where the material is sent to the chaplain, it is the responsibility of the student to contact the chaplain about access to the material. Students may use legal remedies available to them to ensure compliance with the free practice of their religion, but the Tayba Foundation will not be responsible for taking these actions.

2. **Tayba Foundation Correspondence Courses are not meant to be used to undermine other established programs.**
   a. All students must respect the programs of other Muslims and other faith groups.
   b. Students will not make blanket references to staff, volunteers, or other incarcerated prisoners such as "kāfir/infidel," "fāsiq/deviant", "bid'i/innovator." This behavior will not be tolerated.
   c. No material from the Tayba Foundation is to be used to challenge established programs whether they are administered by prison staff, chaplains, volunteers or other incarcerated prisoners.
   d. Students will recognize and respect all established authority figures. This includes, but is not limited to Imams, chaplains, prison administration, and prison staff.
   e. Tayba Foundation will not attempt to resolve issues with staff or other incarcerated prisoners. Students will have to contact appropriate advocacy organizations to find meaningful resolutions to infringement of rights: CAIR, Muslim Advocates, ACLU, etc. In some cases, Tayba can assist the student in finding an appropriate advocacy organization.

3. **Tayba Foundation is non-political.**
   a. We believe that the path to changing our societies is through education and the root of all problems lies in ignorance. Therefore, our solution to the problems comes through educational means and not political means.
   b. Students will not use Tayba Foundation material for political motives.

4. **Tayba Foundation Courses are not meant in any way to be a movement. We are an educational and charitable organization that aims to facilitate educational programs.**
   a. Our course material is not to be used to form any type of unauthorized organization.
   b. Students are not to participate in any group or movement that is illegal or questionable.
   c. Students will not use Tayba Foundation material as part of any unauthorized group.

5. **The Tayba Foundation supports unity.**
   a. Tayba Foundation does not condone use of our material to divide or cause discord within the inmate population or the prison staff. Students must only use our material for the purposes of learning and not create political or social division.
   b. All students will learn to recognize and respect valid differences of opinion.
   c. All students will engage in discussion about the religion in the best of manners. The Qur'ān obliges us to this in the verse, "Do not debate with them except in the best of manners."
   d. The Tayba Foundation's courses are not meant to replace all programs that an inmate may be participating in as our courses are meant to enhance the inmate's learning.
   e. Students should continue any vocational training they are engaged in. A strong work ethic is a must for all Muslims, especially our students.
   f. Students should participate in rehabilitation programs suggested to them by their counselors or administration.

6. **All students will follow their institutional guidelines in regards to all communication with Tayba Foundation.**
   a. Students will not jeopardize Tayba Foundation programs by attempting to communicate in a manner with us that is not allowed by their respective institution's guidelines.
   b. All communication with Tayba Foundation must be in accordance with federal, state and local laws. The Tayba Foundation operates out of Alameda County in California.
   c. Students will not attempt to use Tayba Foundation to relay messages to persons not associated with the organization. This includes other incarcerated prisoners, family, or friends.
   d. Correspondence with Tayba Foundation must only pertain to its educational program.

7. **Students will maintain the highest standard of conduct.**
   a. Students will adhere to the highest standards of ethics and moral behavior.
   b. Tayba Foundation expects all students to behave with integrity and honesty in all their interactions with their prison staff, fellow incarcerated prisoners, family, and community, as well as with Tayba staff.
   c. Tayba Foundation will not be responsible for any inappropriate behavior on the part of its students.
   d. Tayba Foundation strongly condemns religious extremism, intolerance, and any form of terrorism. Students must act in accordance with Tayba's stance on such issues.

Made in the USA
Monee, IL
13 July 2025